Good Poems

BOOKS BY GARRISON KEILLOR

Lake Wobegon Summer 1956
Me: The Jimmy (Big Boy) Valente Story
Wobegon Boy
The Book of Guys
WLT: A Radio Romance
We Are Still Married
Leaving Home
Lake Wobegon Days
Happy to Be Here

Good Poems

Selected and Introduced by

GARRISON KEILLOR

VIKING

VIKING
Published by the Penguin Group
Penguin Putnam Inc., 375 Hudson Street, New York, New York 10014, U.S.A.
Penguin Books Ltd, 80 Strand, London WC2R 0RL, England
Penguin Books Australia Ltd, 250 Camberwell Road, Camberwell, Victoria 3124, Australia
Penguin Books Canada Ltd, 10 Alcorn Avenue, Toronto, Ontario, Canada M4V 3B2
Penguin Books India (P) Ltd, 11 Community Centre, Panchsheel Park, New Delhi–
110 017, India
Penguin Books (N.Z.) Ltd, Cnr Rosedale and Airborne Roads, Albany,
Auckland, New Zealand
Penguin Books (South Africa) (Pty) Ltd, 24 Sturdee Avenue, Rosebank, Johannesburg
2196, South Africa

Penguin Books Ltd, Registered Offices: Harmondsworth, Middlesex, England

First published in 2002 by Viking Penguin, a member of Penguin Putnam Inc.

1   3   5   7   9   10   8   6   4   2

Pages 471–476 constitute an extension of this copyright page.

LIBRARY OF CONGRESS CATALOGING-IN-PUBLICATION DATA
Good poems / selected and introduced by Garrison Keillor.
p.   cm.
ISBN 0-670-03126-7
1. American poetry.   2. English poetry.   I. Keillor, Garrison.
PS586 .G58 2002
811.008—dc21   2002016881

This book is printed on acid-free paper. ∞

Printed in the United States of America

To all the English teachers,
especially the great ones

Contents

Introduction   *xix*

1. O LORD   1

Poem in Thanks   *Thomas Lux*   3
How Many Nights   *Galway Kinnell*   4
Welcome Morning   *Anne Sexton*   5
Psalm 23   from *The Bay*
                                       Psalm Book   7
At Least   *Raymond Carver*   8
Address to the Lord   *John Berryman*   10
O Karma, Dharma, pudding
    and pie   *Philip Appleman*   12
Psalm   *Reed Whittemore*   13
Psalm 121   *Michael Wigglesworth*   14
When one has lived a long
    time alone   *Galway Kinnell*   15
Home on the Range   *Anonymous*   16
What I Want Is   *C. G. Hanzlicek*   18

2. A DAY   21

Summer Morning   *Charles Simic*   23
Otherwise   *Jane Kenyon*   25
Poem About Morning   *William Meredith*   27
Living   *Denise Levertov*   28
Another Spring   *Kenneth Rexroth*   29
Morning Person   *Vassar Miller*   30
Routine   *Arthur Guiterman*   31
The Life of a Day   *Tom Hennen*   32

For My Son, Noah, Ten Years Old	*Robert Bly*	33
I've known a Heaven, like a Tent	*Emily Dickinson*	34
Letter to N.Y.	*Elizabeth Bishop*	35
Dilemma	*David Budbill*	37
from Song of Myself	*Walt Whitman*	38
New Yorkers	*Edward Field*	40
Soaking Up Sun	*Tom Hennen*	41
Late Hours	*Lisel Mueller*	42

3. MUSIC 43

Scrambled Eggs and Whiskey	*Hayden Carruth*	45
Mehitabel's Song	*Don Marquis*	46
Nightclub	*Billy Collins*	48
Alley Violinist	*Robert Lax*	50
Cradle Song	*Jim Schley*	51
Her Door	*Mary Leader*	53
The Pupil	*Donald Justice*	54
Piano	*D. H. Lawrence*	55
Instrument of Choice	*Robert Phillips*	56
Homage: Doo-Wop	*Joseph Stroud*	57
The Persistence of Song	*Howard Moss*	58
Ooly Pop a Cow	*David Huddle*	60
Elevator Music	*Henry Taylor*	62
The Grain of Sound	*Robert Morgan*	63
I Will Make You Brooches	*Robert Louis Stevenson*	64
The Dance	*C. K. Williams*	65
The Investment	*Robert Frost*	66
The Dumka	*B. H. Fairchild*	67
The Green Street Mortuary Marching Band	*Lawrence Ferlinghetti*	69

4. SCENES 71

Poem to Be Read at 3 A.M.	*Donald Justice*	73
The Swimming Pool	*Thomas Lux*	74

Dostoevsky	*Charles Bukowski*	76
After a Movie	*Henry Taylor*	78
Summer Storm	*Dana Gioia*	80
Woolworth's	*Mark Irwin*	82
Worked Late on a Tuesday Night	*Deborah Garrison*	84
The Farmhouse	*Reed Whittemore*	86
wrist-wrestling father	*Orval Lund*	88
Yorkshiremen in Pub Gardens	*Gavin Ewart*	89
Noah	*Roy Daniells*	90

5. LOVERS   91

A Red, Red Rose	*Robert Burns*	93
When I Heard at the Close of Day	*Walt Whitman*	94
First Love	*John Clare*	95
He Wishes for the Cloths of Heaven	*W. B. Yeats*	96
Sonnet	*C. B. Trail*	97
Politics	*W. B. Yeats*	98
Magellan Street, 1974	*Maxine Kumin*	99
Animals	*Frank O'Hara*	101
Lending Out Books	*Hal Sirowitz*	102
The Changed Man	*Robert Phillips*	103
The Constant North	*J. F. Hendry*	105
On the Strength of All Conviction and the Stamina of Love	*Jennifer Michael Hecht*	106
The Loft	*Richard Jones*	107
This Is Just to Say	*William Carlos Williams*	109
This Is Just to Say	*Erica-Lynn Gambino*	110
Venetian Air	*Thomas Moore*	111
Summer Morning	*Louis Simpson*	112
Comin thro' the Rye	*Robert Burns*	113

Topography	*Sharon Olds*	114
Saturday Morning	*Hugo Williams*	115
Flight	*Louis Jenkins*	116
At Twenty-Three Weeks She Can No Longer See Anything South of Her Belly	*Thom Ward*	117
For the Life of Him and Her	*Reed Whittemore*	119
Romantics	*Lisel Mueller*	120
Down in the Valley	*Anonymous*	122
The Middle Years	*Walter McDonald*	124
Winter Winds Cold and Blea . . .	*John Clare*	126
since feeling is first	*e. e. cummings*	127
Vergissmeinnicht	*Keith Douglas*	128
Sonnet XLIII What lips my lips have kissed	*Edna St. Vincent Millay*	130
After the Argument	*Stephen Dunn*	131
The Orange	*Wendy Cope*	133
Susquehanna	*Liz Rosenberg*	134
Farm Wife	*R. S. Thomas*	135
After Forty Years of Marriage, She Tries a New Recipe for Hamburger Hot Dish	*Leo Dangel*	136
Those Who Love	*Sara Teasdale*	137
Quietly	*Kenneth Rexroth*	138
For C.W.B.	*Elizabeth Bishop*	139
Shorelines	*Howard Moss*	141
Prayer for a Marriage	*Steve Scafidi*	143
The Master Speed	*Robert Frost*	145
Bonnard's Nudes	*Raymond Carver*	146

6. DAY'S WORK — 147

Happiness	*Raymond Carver*	149
Hoeing	*John Updike*	150

Some Details of Hebridean House Construction	Thomas A. Clark	151
Relations	Philip Booth	153
What I Learned from My Mother	Julia Kasdorf	156
To be of use	Marge Piercy	157
No Tool or Rope or Pail	Bob Arnold	159
Ox Cart Man	Donald Hall	161
Girl on a Tractor	Joyce Sutphen	163
Soybeans	Thomas Alan Orr	164
Landing Pattern	Philip Appleman	166
Mae West	Edward Field	168
Hay for the Horses	Gary Snyder	170

7. SONS AND DAUGHTERS

		171
Masterworks of Ming	Kay Ryan	173
Bess	Linda Pastan	175
A Little Tooth	Thomas Lux	176
Sonnet XXXVII	William Shakespeare	177
Egg	C. G. Hanzlicek	178
Rolls-Royce Dreams	Ginger Andrews	180
My Life Before I Knew It	Lawrence Raab	181
After Work	Richard Jones	183
I Stop Writing the Poem	Tess Gallagher	184
Franklin Hyde	Hilaire Belloc	185
Manners	Elizabeth Bishop	186
September, the First Day of School	Howard Nemerov	188
First Lesson	Philip Booth	190
Childhood	Barbara Ras	191
Waving Good-Bye	Gerald Stern	193
Family Reunion	Maxine Kumin	194

8. LANGUAGE   197

A Primer of the Daily Round   *Howard Nemerov*   199
The Possessive Case   *Lisel Mueller*   200
The Icelandic Language   *Bill Holm*   202
The Fantastic Names of Jazz   *Hayden Carruth*   204
Ode to the Medieval Poets   *W. H. Auden*   205
Sweater Weather   *Sharon Bryan*   207

9. A GOOD LIFE   209

We grow accustomed to
  the Dark—   *Emily Dickinson*   211
A Ritual to Read to Each Other   *William Stafford*   212
Courage   *Anne Sexton*   213
Sometimes   *Sheenagh Pugh*   215
Leisure   *W. H. Davies*   216
the way it is now   *Charles Bukowski*   217
A Secret Life   *Stephen Dunn*   218
Lost   *David Wagoner*   219
Sonnet XXV   *William Shakespeare*   220
The Eel in the Cave   *Robert Bly*   221
Wild Geese   *Mary Oliver*   222
From the Manifesto of the
  Selfish   *Stephen Dunn*   223
Hope   *Lisel Mueller*   224
The Three Goals   *David Budbill*   225
Vermeer   *Howard Nemerov*   226
Repression   *C. K. Williams*   227
Weather   *Linda Pastan*   228
Moderation Is Not a Negation
  of Intensity, But Helps Avoid
  Monotony   *John Tagliabue*   229
Tell all the Truth but tell it slant *Emily Dickinson*   230
The Props assist the House . . .   *Emily Dickinson*   231

10. BEASTS

		233
Little Citizen, Little Survivor	*Hayden Carruth*	235
Her First Calf	*Wendell Berry*	236
Bats	*Randall Jarrell*	237
Riding Lesson	*Henry Taylor*	239
Walking the Dog	*Howard Nemerov*	240
The Excrement Poem	*Maxine Kumin*	241
Stanza IV *from* Coming of Age	*Ursula Leguin*	243
Destruction	*Joanne Kyger*	244
How to See Deer	*Philip Booth*	245
Dog's Death	*John Updike*	247
Names of Horses	*Donald Hall*	248
Bison Crossing Near Mt. Rushmore	*May Swenson*	250

11. FAILURE

		251
Success is counted sweetest . . .	*Emily Dickinson*	253
Solitude	*Ella Wheeler Wilcox*	254
The first time I remember	*Wendell Berry*	255
Our Lady of the Snows	*Robert Hass*	256
The British Museum Reading Room	*Louis MacNeice*	257
The Bare Arms of Trees	*John Tagliabue*	258
The Sailor	*Geof Hewitt*	259
A Place for Everything	*Louis Jenkins*	260
The Feast	*Robert Hass*	261
Nobody Knows You	*Jimmie Cox*	262
the last song	*Charles Bukowski*	263

12. COMPLAINT

		265
The Forsaken Wife	*Elizabeth Thomas*	267
Confession	*Stephen Dobyns*	268
Living in the Body	*Joyce Sutphen*	269

Tired As I Can Be	Bessie Jackson	270
The Iceberg Theory	Gerald Locklin	272
Manifesto: The Mad Farmer Liberation Front	Wendell Berry	274
A Bookmark	Tom Disch	276
poetry readings	Charles Bukowski	277
Publication—is the Auction . . .	Emily Dickinson	279

13. TRIPS — 281

Once in the 40s	William Stafford	283
lines from Moby Dick	Herman Melville	284
Rain Travel	W. S. Merwin	285
where we are	Gerald Locklin	286
Excelsior	Henry Wadsworth Longfellow	287
On a Tree Fallen Across the Road	Robert Frost	289
A Walk Along the Old Tracks	Robert Kinsley	290
Passengers	Billy Collins	291
The Walloping Window-Blind	Charles Edward Carryl	293
The Vacation	Wendell Berry	295
Directions	Joseph Stroud	296
Postscript	Seamus Heaney	297
Night Journey	Theodore Roethke	298
Waiting	Raymond Carver	299

14. SNOW — 301

New Hampshire	Howard Moss	303
To fight aloud . . .	Emily Dickinson	305
December Moon	May Sarton	306
Year's End	Richard Wilbur	307
The Snow Man	Wallace Stevens	309
January	Baron Wormser	310
in celebration of surviving	Chuck Miller	312
Her Long Illness	Donald Hall	313

Requiescat	*Oscar Wilde*	314
The Sixth of January	*David Budbill*	315
Not Only the Eskimos	*Lisel Mueller*	316
Boy at the Window	*Richard Wilbur*	319
Winter Poem	*Frederick Morgan*	320
Lester Tells of Wanda and the Big Snow	*Paul Zimmer*	321
Old Boards	*Robert Bly*	322
March Blizzard	*John Tagliabue*	323

15. YELLOW — 325

Elvis Kissed Me	*T. S. Kerrigan*	327
Stepping Out of Poetry	*Gerald Stern*	328
I shall keep singing!	*Emily Dickinson*	329
Song to Onions	*Roy Blount, Jr.*	330
O Luxury	*Guy W. Longchamps*	332
Coming	*Kenneth Rexroth*	334
A Light Left On	*May Sarton*	335
The Yellow Slicker	*Stuart Dischell*	336
First Kiss	*April Lindner*	337
The Music One Looks Back On	*Stephen Dobyns*	338

16. LIVES — 341

In a Prominent Bar in Secaucus One Day	*X. J. Kennedy*	343
Who's Who	*W. H. Auden*	345
The Portrait	*Stanley Kunitz*	346
Parable of the Four-Poster	*Erica Jong*	347
Ed	*Louis Simpson*	349
Memory	*Hayden Carruth*	350
Lazy	*David Lee*	351
Testimonial	*Harry Newman, Jr.*	354
Cathedral Builders	*John Ormond*	356
The Village Burglar	*Anonymous*	357

The Scandal	Robert Bly	358
At Last the Secret Is Out	W. H. Auden	359
Night Light	Kate Barnes	360
Sir Patrick Spens	Anonymous	361

17. ELDERS 365

I Go Back to May 1937	Sharon Olds	367
Those Winter Sundays	Robert Hayden	369
The Old Liberators	Robert Hedin	370
To My Mother	Wendell Berry	371
Working in the Rain	Robert Morgan	373
Birthday Card to My Mother	Philip Appleman	374
Yesterday	W. S. Merwin	376
No Map	Stephen Dobyns	378
My Mother	Robert Mezey	379
When My Dead Father Called	Robert Bly	381
August Third	May Sarton	382
Terminus	Ralph Waldo Emerson	384

18. THE END 387

Authorship	James B(all) Naylor	389
Young and Old	Charles Kingsley	390
Shifting the Sun	Diana Der-Hovanessian	391
My Dad's Wallet	Raymond Carver	393
When I Am Asked	Lisel Mueller	396
Dirge Without Music	Edna St. Vincent Millay	397
My mother said . . .	Donald Hall	398
Departures	Linda Pastan	399
As Befits a Man	Langston Hughes	400
Sunt Leones	Stevie Smith	401
Perfection Wasted	John Updike	402
Eleanor's Letters	Donald Hall	403
Death and the Turtle	May Sarton	404
Four Poems in One	Anne Porter	405

Titanic   David R. Slavitt   407
The Burial of Sir John
  Moore after Corunna   Charles Wolfe   408
Kaddish   David Ignatow   410
Twilight: After Haying   Jane Kenyon   411
For the Anniversary of My Death   W. S. Merwin   413
from The Old Italians Dying   Lawrence Ferlinghetti   414
Street Ballad   George Barker   416
Let Evening Come   Jane Kenyon   417

19. THE RESURRECTION   419

Forty-Five   Hayden Carruth   421
A Blessing   James Wright   422
Holy Thursday   William Blake   423
lines from Walden   Henry David Thoreau   424
The Peace of Wild Things   Wendell Berry   426
From Blossoms   Li-Young Lee   427
The First Green of Spring   David Budbill   428
Here   Grace Paley   429
The Lives of the Heart   Jane Hirshfield   430
Spring   Gerard Manley Hopkins   432
Fishing in the Keep of Silence   Linda Gregg   433

Biographies   435
Name Index   463
Title Index   467

Introduction

This is not *Introduction to Poetry* (*MWF 9am Chemistry 150, 3 cr*) and I am not the Maud Hill Hallowell Professor of American Lit, and your name isn't Daphne Foxcroft. It's simply a book of poems that got read over the radio on a daily five-minute show called *The Writer's Almanac*, poems that somehow stuck with me and with some of the listeners. Stickiness, memorability, is one sign of a good poem. You hear it and a day later some of it is still there in the brainpan.

The goodness of a poem is severely tested by reading it on the radio. The radio audience is not the devout sisterhood you find at poetry readings, leaning forward, lips pursed, hanky in hand; it's more like a high school cafeteria. People listen to poems while they're frying eggs and sausage and reading the paper and reasoning with their offspring, so I find it wise to stay away from stuff that is too airy or that refers off-handedly to the poet Li-Po or relies on your familiarity with butterflies or Spanish or Monet.

Most listeners are otherwise engaged—we in radio know this; mostly we're a backdrop to bigger things, like the palace guard in *Aida*, the surf on the sound machine, a sort of prayer wheel. But sometimes a poem cuts through the static and delivers some good thing. It is of use; it gives value. James Wright's "A Blessing" was heard by a woman on her Walkman while hustling down a concourse at the Dallas/Fort Worth airport and she stopped to listen to it, though a moment before she had been rushing to catch a plane, and to be interrupted mid-stampede by a beautiful thing is a blessing indeed. Wright's poem about himself and his friend climbing through barbed wire to visit two horses in a pasture is one that gets read at weddings and memorial services, has been done in needlework and carved into wood, and appears on a brass plaque at an interstate rest stop near Rochester, Minnesota. W. S. Merwin says, "If a poem is not forgotten as soon as the circumstances of its origin, it begins at once to evolve an existence of its own, in minds and lives, and then even in words, that its singular maker could never have imagined." And so Wright's poem has: it has made its way in the world, a good poem, and found its way and touched people and been used in ceremonies, as a friendly benediction.

To see poetry finding an existence that its maker never imagined, visit Emily Dickinson's grave in Amherst. Here lies the white-gowned virgin goddess, in a cluster of Dickinsons, under a stone that says "Called Back," and here, weekly, strangers come as grieving family, placing pebbles on her big stone, leaving notes to her folded into tiny squares, under small stones. Dickinson was a famous recluse who camped in the shadows in the upstairs hall and eavesdropped on visitors, and now there are few graves in America so venerated as hers. She is mourned continually because the quickness and vitality of her poems make her contemporary, and when you make flies buzz and horses turn their heads and you declaim *Wild Nights! Wild Nights!* and give hope some feathers, you are going to have friends in this world for as long as English is read.

Oblivion is the writer's greatest fear, and as with the fear of death, one finds evidence to support it. You fear that your work, the work of your lifetime, on which you labored so unspeakably hard and for which you stood on so many rocky shores and thought, *My life has been wasted utterly*—your work will have its brief shining moment, the band plays, some confetti is tossed, you are photographed with your family, drinks are served, people squeeze your hand and say that you seem to have lost weight, and then the work languishes in the bookstore and dies and is remaindered and

finally entombed on a shelf and—*nobody ever looks at it again! Nobody!*
This happens rather often, actually. Life is intense and the printed
page is so faint. Billy Collins wrote (in his poem, "Forgetfulness"):

> *The name of the author is the first to go*
> *followed obediently by the title, the plot,*
> *the heartbreaking conclusion, the entire novel*
> *which suddenly becomes one you have never read,*
> *never even heard of.*

When the reader does not forget, when the reader has even
committed the poem to memory and can quote it years later, this
is a triumph of large proportions.

What makes a poem memorable is its narrative line. A story is
easier to remember than a puzzle. (And there are rules in storytelling that make for a better poem: Stop Mumbling, No Prefaces,
Cut to the Chase, Don't Sound Like a Writer, Be Real.)

Good poems tend to incorporate some story, some cadence or
shadow of story. There is a story in Dickinson's *Success is counted
sweetest by those who ne'er succeed* and Shakespeare's *When in disgrace
with fortune and men's eyes* and Wright's *Just off the highway to Rochester,
Minnesota/Twilight bounds softly forth on the grass./And the eyes of those two
Indian ponies/Darken with kindness* and Oliver's *You do not have to be
good./You do not have to walk on your knees/For a hundred miles through the
desert, repenting.* And Merwin's "For the Anniversary of My Death"
(*Every year without knowing it I have passed the day/When the last fires will
wave to me.*) You could, without much trouble, commit these poems
to memory and have them by heart, like a cello in your head, a
portable beauty to steady you and ward off despair.

Raymond Carver said, "Whether I am writing a poem or writing prose, I am still trying to tell a story." Kenneth Rexroth called
on poets to write about "real things that happen to real people"
and when a critic referred to him as one of the bearshit-on-the-
trail nature poets, Rexroth took it as an honor. Dana Gioia said,

"When poets stopped telling stories, they not only lost a substantial portion of their audience; they also narrowed the imaginative possibilities of their art. As long as there have been poets, those poets told stories. Those stories were rarely about their own lives but about imagined lives—drawn from myth, legend, history, or current events."

I looked at a truckload of poems to find the few thousand I've read on the radio, and it's an education. First of all, most poems aren't memorable; in fact, they make no impression at all. Sorry, but it's true. There are brave blurbs on the back cover ("writes with a lyrical luminosity that reconceptualizes experience with cognitive beauty") but you open up the goods and they're like condoms on the beach, evidence that somebody was here once and had an experience but not of great interest to the passerby.

Sometimes, however, one is dead wrong. I've come to admire writers I once cocked a snoot at, like Raymond Carver and Charles Bukowski. Bukowski said, "There is nothing wrong with poetry that is entertaining and easy to understand. Genius could be the ability to say a profound thing in a simple way." This is not what an English major like me cared to hear, back when I was busy writing poems that were lacerating, opaque, complexly layered, unreadable. But now I'm older and I read Bukowski's love poems, his odes to companionship and city scenes and nightlife, and admire his good humor, e.g., the poem in which he says he's lived with some fine women in his time but he would rather drive in reverse gear from L.A. to N.Y. than live with any of them again, and I wonder, Why do English teachers offer their prisoners so much Cummings and no Bukowski? Why do standard anthologies include one and never mention the other? Because one of them went to Harvard and had fine manners and lived in the Village, around the corner from the publisher, and the other was a day laborer and roughneck who lived in L.A. and had bad skin and looked like a gargoyle, that's why.

And then there is T. S. Eliot, the great stuffed owl whose glassy eyes mesmerized the English profs of my day. Eliot was once a cultural icon, the American guy so smooth he passed for British, and when he came to Minneapolis on tour in the mid-fifties, he practically filled a basketball arena; he was a bigger draw than Frost, *Prufrock* being required reading in the eleventh grade, but you look at his work today and it seems rather bloodless next to, say, Rexroth's. Eliot didn't get out of the house much while Rexroth was dancing all over town. Anybody who would rather read *Ash Wednesday* than Rexroth's love poems must be on the take. And yet Rexroth was never mentioned in the halls of the English Department when I was there, nor was Ferlinghetti, that great-hearted, God-gifted man. His City Lights bookstore has always been a mecca in San Francisco. His friend Allen Ginsberg, on the other hand, a good man, admirable in so many ways (especially for *Kaddish*), was something of a gasbag, not big on rewriting, and reading his *Collected Poems* is like hiking across North Dakota. I stopped just beyond Fargo.

I expected to include plenty of Whitman here and discovered, reading him, a sort of seasickness at all those undulating lines of Uncle Walt's perpetual swoon over grass and leaves and camera-dos. There are good poems there, and it's a mistake to omit them, but Walt is the Typhoid Mary of American Lit: so much bad poetry can be traced back to him (and not brief bad poems, either), he gave so many dreadful writers permission to lavish themselves upon us. Lord, forgive me.

Howard Nemerov seems larger and larger to me with each rereading, a kindly giant of great courage and elegance. I admire the industrious and illustrious Auden, the conscientious W. C. Williams. Elizabeth Bishop, William Stafford, Robert Bly: Emily would have perused them with pleasure. Bly is still with us, 75, writing at top form, and this gives hope to the rest of us. It was a rich generation, born in the mid-twenties: Bly and Wright, Simpson, Stern, O'Hara,

Justice, Kumin, Moss, Paley, Sexton, Adrienne Rich, John Ashbery. Great men like W. S. Merwin on his palm plantation in Maui, sturdy and cheerful, a writer who has made his own way brilliantly and with great resourcefulness. Donald Hall, still throwing strikes in his old age. My generation of pre-boomers seems light in the loafers compared to the Seniors, a lacrosse team as opposed to the New York Giants, but we do have Carver and Dana Gioia and Billy Collins, the current Poet Laureate and Serene Master and Blissful Poobah, a New York guy who makes people laugh and who teaches literature to welfare mothers, God bless him.

If you read a lot, labels start to seem meaningless. "Regional," for example, which only means writers whose work might include references to farming, is a useless term. Likewise, "confessional" poetry. And that dreary term, "light verse," which banishes humor like an insane uncle to the back bedroom. "Women's lit" strikes me as one of the great dumb ideas to come out of my generation, right up there with multiculturalism. Elizabeth Bishop was a woman, ditto Emily Dickinson, and she can take your head off with one line, too, but if you marshal women writers under one tent, comparisons are inevitable, and the occupants will not be content for long. When you compare Bishop to, say, her friend and mentor Marianne Moore, the mentor pales severely. Marianne Moore was a dotty old aunt whose poems are quite replicable for anyone with a thesaurus. A nice lady, but definitely a plodder, and it would be cruel punishment to have to write a book about her. Her contemporary, Edna St. Vincent Millay, who played the glamorous broad and taxi dancer to Moore's bunhead librarian, wrote more that is still of interest, whereas Moore's reputation must be due to the fact that, in the republic of letters, there are many more Moores than Millays. From Millay it's a straight shot to Anne Sexton, a writer of profound exuberance and wit and a hot number, and her cohort, the beautiful horsekeeper, Maxine Kumin, two women who, forgive me, make St. Sylvia look like tuna salad. Plath is a small dark cloud and Kumin and Sexton are writers you can take anywhere. You could read them at the beach, in blazing sunlight, and your attention would not drift.

What makes Kumin and Sexton matter, and makes all good poems matter, is that they offer a truer account than what we're used to getting. They surprise us with clear pictures of the familiar. The soft arc of an afternoon in a few lines. Poems that make us love this gaudy, mother-scented, mud-bedaubed language of ours. A cunning low tongue, English, with its rich vocabulary of slander and concupiscence and sport, its fine Latin overlay and French bric-a-brac, and when someone speaks poetry in it, it stirs our little monolingual hearts.

The love of language is the love of truth, and this brings one into conflict with authority, since power employs deceit and is so fond of it—Rexroth said: "The accepted official version of anything is most likely false . . . all authority is based on fraud"—but the love of language is a fundamental connection to our fellows and is a basis of true civility. Stafford wrote:

> *If you don't know the kind of person I am*
> *And I don't know the kind of person you are*
> *A pattern that others made may prevail in the world*
> *And following the wrong god home we may miss our star.*

As to what kind of person you are, Rexroth said, "The mature man lives quietly, does good privately, assumes personal responsibility for his actions, treats others with friendliness and courtesy, finds mischief boring and keeps out of it. Without this hidden conspiracy of good will, society would not endure an hour."

And that is the hidden subtitle of this book: a conspiracy of friendliness. "Good poem" may seem faint praise compared to the blurbish terms *brilliant, luminous, powerful,* etc., but among friends, it's all the compliment you'd ever need or want.

The pleasure of making this book is the chance to put poets such as Jennifer Michael Hecht and C. G. Hanzlicek and April Lindner and Ginger Andrews and Louis Jenkins into a club with Frost and Dickinson and Burns and Shakespeare.

The pain of it is to look at the book and realize who I left out who should've been here. I can think of a dozen without hesitation. I am sorry for the omissions.

But I hope that the includees know that their poems mean a lot to people. These are poems that made people stop chewing their toasted muffins and turn up the radio and listen and later zip into our website and get the dope on the poet. Many of these poems have been deeply loved by people, and why not? They deserve to be.

Raymond Carver wrote:

> *And did you get what*
> *you wanted from this life, even so?*
> *I did.*
> *And what did you want?*
> *To call myself beloved, to feel myself*
> *beloved on the earth.*

> —G.K.

Kathy Roach and Kay Gornick contributed mightily to making this book, and so did Brett Kelly and Molly Stern. And thanks to Hadassah Heins.

Good Poems

1

O LORD

Poem in Thanks

Thomas Lux

Lord Whoever, thank you for this air
I'm about to in- and exhale, this hutch
in the woods, the wood for fire,
the light—both lamp and the natural stuff
of leaf-back, fern, and wing.
For the piano, the shovel
for ashes, the moth-gnawed
blankets, the stone-cold water
stone-cold: thank you.
Thank you, Lord, coming for
to carry me here—where I'll gnash
it out, Lord, where I'll calm
and work, Lord, thank you
for the goddamn birds singing!

How Many Nights

Galway Kinnell

How many nights
have I lain in terror,
O Creator Spirit, Maker of night and day,

only to walk out
the next morning over the frozen world
hearing under the creaking of snow
faint, peaceful breaths . . .
snake,
bear, earthworm, ant . . .

and above me
a wild crow crying 'yaw yaw yaw'
from a branch nothing cried from ever in my life.

Welcome Morning

Anne Sexton

There is joy
in all:
in the hair I brush each morning,
in the Cannon towel, newly washed,
that I rub my body with each morning,
in the chapel of eggs I cook
each morning,
in the outcry from the kettle
that heats my coffee
each morning,
in the spoon and the chair
that cry "hello there, Anne"
each morning,
in the godhead of the table
that I set my silver, plate, cup upon
each morning.

All this is God,
right here in my pea-green house
each morning
and I mean,
though often forget,
to give thanks,
to faint down by the kitchen table
in a prayer of rejoicing

as the holy birds at the kitchen window
peck into their marriage of seeds.

So while I think of it,
let me paint a thank-you on my palm
for this God, this laughter of the morning,
lest it go unspoken.

The Joy that isn't shared, I've heard,
dies young.

Psalm 23

from *The Bay Psalm Book*

The Lord to me a shepherd is,
    want therefore shall not I:
He in the folds of tender grass,
    doth cause me down to lie:
To waters calm me gently leads
    restore my soul doth he:
He doth in paths of righteousness
    for his name's sake lead me.
Yea, though in valley of death's shade
    I walk, none ill I'll fear:
Because thou art with me, thy rod,
    and staff my comfort are.
For me a table thou hast spread,
    in presence of my foes:
Thou dost anoint my head with oil;
    my cup it overflows.
Goodness and mercy surely shall
    all my days follow me:
And in the Lord's house I shall dwell
    so long as days shall be.

At Least

Raymond Carver

I want to get up early one more morning,
before sunrise. Before the birds, even.
I want to throw cold water on my face
and be at my work table
when the sky lightens and smoke
begins to rise from the chimneys
of the other houses.
I want to see the waves break
on this rocky beach, not just hear them
break as I did all night in my sleep.
I want to see again the ships
that pass through the Strait from every
seafaring country in the world—
old, dirty freighters just barely moving along,
and the swift new cargo vessels
painted every color under the sun
that cut the water as they pass.
I want to keep an eye out for them.
And for the little boat that plies
the water between the ships
and the pilot station near the lighthouse.
I want to see them take a man off the ship
and put another up on board.
I want to spend the day watching this happen
and reach my own conclusions.
I hate to seem greedy—I have so much

to be thankful for already.
But I want to get up early one more morning, at least.
And go to my place with some coffee and wait.
Just wait, to see what's going to happen.

Address to the Lord

John Berryman

1
Master of beauty, craftsman of the snowflake,
inimitable contriver,
endower of Earth so gorgeous & different from the boring Moon,
thank you for such as it is my gift.

I have made up a morning prayer to you
containing with precision everything that most matters.
'According to Thy will' the thing begins.
It took me off & on two days. It does not aim at eloquence.

You have come to my rescue again & again
in my impassable, sometimes despairing years.
You have allowed my brilliant friends to destroy themselves
and I am still here, severely damaged, but functioning.

Unknowable, as I am unknown to my guinea pigs:
How can I 'love' you?
I only as far as gratitude & awe
confidently & absolutely go.

I have no idea whether we live again.
It doesn't seem likely
from either the scientific or the philosophical point of view
but certainly all things are possible to you,

and I believe as fixedly in the Resurrection-appearances to Peter
    and

                                                    to Paul

            as I believe I sit in this blue chair.
Only that may have been a special case
to establish their initiatory faith.

Whatever your end may be, accept my amazement.
May I stand until death forever at attention
for any your least instruction or enlightenment.
I even feel sure you will assist me again, Master of insight & beauty.

Philip Appleman

O Karma, Dharma, pudding and pie,
gimme a break before I die:
grant me wisdom, will, & wit,
purity, probity, pluck, & grit.
Trustworthy, loyal, helpful, kind,
gimme great abs & a steel-trap mind,
and forgive, Ye Gods, some humble advice—
these little blessings would suffice
to beget an earthly paradise:
make the bad people good—
and the good people nice;
and before our world goes over the brink,
teach the believers how to think.

Psalm

Reed Whittemore

The Lord feeds some of His prisoners better than others.
It could be said of Him that He is not a just god but an
　　indifferent god.
That He is not to be trusted to reward the righteous and
　　punish the unscrupulous.
That He maketh the poor poorer but is otherwise
　　undependable.

It could be said of Him that it is His school of the germane
　　that produced the *Congressional Record.*
That it is His vision of justice that gave us cost accounting.

It could be said of Him that though we walk with Him all
　　the days of our lives we will never fathom Him
Because He is empty.

These are the dark images of our Lord
That make it seem needful for us to pray not unto Him
But ourselves.
But when we do that we find that indeed we are truly lost
And we rush back into the safer fold, impressed by His care
　　for us.

Psalm 121

Michael Wigglesworth

I to the hills lift up mine eyes,
 from whence shall come mine aid.
Mine help doth from Jehovah come,
 which heaven and earth hath made.
He will not let thy foot be moved,
 nor slumber; that thee keeps.
Lo, he that keepeth Israel,
 he slumbreth not, nor sleeps.
The Lord thy keeper is, the Lord
 on thy right hand the shade.
The sun by day, nor moon by night,
 shall thee by stroke invade.
The Lord will keep thee from all ill:
 thy soul he keeps alway,
Thy going out and thy income,
 the Lord keeps now and aye.

Galway Kinnell

When one has lived a long time alone,
and the hermit thrush calls and there is an answer,
and the bullfrog head half out of water utters
the cantillations he sang in his first spring,
and the snake lowers himself over the threshold
and creeps away among the stones, one sees
they all live to mate with their kind, and one knows,
after a long time of solitude, after the many steps taken
away from one's kind, toward these other kingdoms,
the hard prayer inside one's own singing
is to come back, if one can, to one's own,
a world almost lost, in the exile that deepens,
when one has lived a long time alone.

Home on the Range

Anonymous

There's a land in the West where nature is blessed
With a beauty so vast and austere,
And though you have flown off to cities unknown,
Your memories bring you back here.

Home, home on the range
Where the deer and the antelope play.
Where seldom is heard a discouraging word
And the skies are not cloudy all day.

Where the air is so pure, the zephyrs so free,
The breezes so balmy and light,
That I would not exchange my home on the range
For all of the cities so bright.

How often at night when the heavens are bright
With the light of the glittering stars,
Have I stood here amazed and asked as I gazed
If their glory exceeds that of ours.

Where the teepees were raised in a cool shady place
By the rivers where sweet grasses grew
Where the bison was found on the great hunting ground
And fed all the nations of Sioux.

The canyons and buttes like old twisted roots
And the sandstone of ancient stream beds
In the sunset they rise to dazzle our eyes
With their lavenders, yellows, and reds.

Oh, give me a land where the bright diamond sand
Flows leisurely down to the stream;
Where the graceful white swan goes gliding along
Like a maid in a heavenly dream.

When it comes my time to leave this world behind
And fly off to regions unknown,
Please lay my remains on the great plains,
Out in my sweet prairie home.

Home, home on the plains
Here in the grass we will lie
When our day's work is done by the light of the sun
As it sets in the blue prairie sky.

What I Want Is

C. G. Hanzlicek

What I want is
Enough money

To have what I want
What I want is

My own hill
And beneath that hill

A pond
In the pond a lazy

Bass or two
And duck feathers

Resting on the mud
Of the shore

Between the hill
And mud a patch

Of grass where I
Can lie and count

My seven trees
My seven clouds

And count the coyotes
Coming down the hill

To drink
Coyote 1 Coyote 2

2

A DAY

Summer Morning

Charles Simic

I love to stay in bed
All morning,
Covers thrown off, naked,
Eyes closed, listening.

Outside they are opening
Their primers
In the little school
Of the cornfield.

There's a smell of damp hay,
Of horses, laziness,
Summer sky and eternal life.

I know all the dark places
Where the sun hasn't reached yet,
Where the last cricket
Has just hushed; anthills
Where it sounds like it's raining;
Slumbering spiders spinning wedding dresses.

I pass over the farmhouses
Where the little mouths open to suck,
Barnyards where a man, naked to the waist,
Washes his face and shoulders with a hose,
Where the dishes begin to rattle in the kitchen.

The good tree with its voice
Of a mountain stream
Knows my steps.
It, too, hushes.

I stop and listen:
Somewhere close by
A stone cracks a knuckle,
Another turns over in its sleep.

I hear a butterfly stirring
Inside a caterpillar.
I hear the dust talking
Of last night's storm.

Farther ahead, someone
Even more silent
Passes over the grass
Without bending it.

And all of a sudden:
In the midst of that quiet,
It seems possible
To live simply on this earth.

Otherwise

Jane Kenyon

I got out of bed
on two strong legs.
It might have been
otherwise. I ate
cereal, sweet
milk, ripe, flawless
peach. It might
have been otherwise.
I took the dog uphill
to the birch wood.
All morning I did
the work I love.

At noon I lay down
with my mate. It might
have been otherwise.
We ate dinner together
at a table with silver
candlesticks. It might
have been otherwise.
I slept in a bed
in a room with paintings
on the walls, and

planned another day
just like this day.
But one day, I know,
it will be otherwise.

Poem About Morning

William Meredith

Whether it's sunny or not, it's sure
To be enormously complex—
Trees or streets outdoors, indoors whoever you share,
And yourself, thirsty, hungry, washing,
An attitude towards sex.
No wonder half of you wants to stay
With your head dark and wishing
Rather than take it all on again:
Weren't you duped yesterday?
Things are not orderly here, no matter what they say.

But the clock goes off, if you have a dog
It wags, if you get up now you'll be less
Late. Life is some kind of loathsome hag
Who is forever threatening to turn beautiful.
Now she gives you a quick toothpaste kiss
And puts a glass of cold cranberry juice,
Like a big fake garnet, in your hand.
Cranberry juice! You're lucky, on the whole,
But there is a great deal about it you don't understand.

Living

Denise Levertov

The fire in leaf and grass
so green it seems
each summer the last summer.

The wind blowing, the leaves
shivering in the sun,
each day the last day.

A red salamander
so cold and so
easy to catch, dreamily

moves his delicate feet
and long tail. I hold
my hand open for him to go.

Each minute the last minute.

Another Spring

Kenneth Rexroth

The seasons revolve and the years change
With no assistance or supervision.
The moon, without taking thought,
Moves in its cycle, full, crescent, and full.

The white moon enters the heart of the river;
The air is drugged with azalea blossoms;
Deep in the night a pine cone falls;
Our campfire dies out in the empty mountains.

The sharp stars flicker in the tremulous branches;
The lake is black, bottomless in the crystalline night;
High in the sky the Northern Crown
Is cut in half by the dim summit of a snow peak.

O heart, heart, so singularly
Intransigent and corruptible,
Here we lie entranced by the starlit water,
And moments that should each last forever

Slide unconsciously by us like water.

Morning Person

Vassar Miller

God, best at making in the morning, tossed
stars and planets, singing and dancing, rolled
Saturn's rings spinning and humming, twirled the earth
so hard it coughed and spat the moon up, brilliant
bubble floating around it for good, stretched holy
hands till birds in nervous sparks flew forth from
them and beasts—lizards, big and little, apes,
lions, elephants, dogs and cats cavorting,
tumbling over themselves, dizzy with joy when
God made us in the morning too, both man
and woman, leaving Adam no time for
sleep so nimbly was Eve bouncing out of
his side till as night came everything and
everybody, growing tired, declined, sat
down in one soft descended Hallelujah.

Routine

Arthur Guiterman

No matter what we are and who,
Some duties everyone must do:

A Poet puts aside his wreath
To wash his face and brush his teeth,

  And even Earls
  Must comb their curls,

  And even Kings
  Have underthings.

The Life of a Day

Tom Hennen

Like people or dogs, each day is unique and has
its own personality quirks which can easily be seen
if you look closely. But there are so few days as
compared to people, not to mention dogs, that it
would be surprising if a day were not a hundred
times more interesting than most people. But
usually they just pass, mostly unnoticed, unless
they are wildly nice, like autumn ones full of red
maple trees and hazy sunlight, or if they are grimly
awful ones in a winter blizzard that kills the lost
traveler and bunches of cattle. For some reason
we like to see days pass, even though most of us
claim we don't want to reach our last one for a
long time. We examine each day before us with
barely a glance and say, no, this isn't one I've been
looking for, and wait in a bored sort of way for
the next, when, we are convinced, our lives will
start for real. Meanwhile, this day is going by perfectly well-adjusted, as some days are, with the
right amounts of sunlight and shade, and a light
breeze scented with a perfume made from the
mixture of fallen apples, corn stubble, dry oak
leaves, and the faint odor of last night's meander-
ing skunk.

For My Son, Noah, Ten Years Old

Robert Bly

Night and day arrive, and day after day goes by,
and what is old remains old, and what is young remains
    young, and grows old,
and the lumber pile does not grow younger, nor the
    weathered two by fours lose their darkness,
but the old tree goes on, the barn stands without help so
    many years,
the advocate of darkness and night is not lost.

The horse swings around on one leg, steps, and turns,
the chicken flapping claws onto the roost, its wings whelping
    and whalloping,
but what is primitive is not to be shot out into the night and
    the dark.
And slowly the kind man comes closer, loses his rage, sits
    down at table.

So I am proud only of those days that we pass in undivided
    tenderness,
when you sit drawing, or making books, stapled, with
    messages to the world . . .
or coloring a man with fire coming out of his hair.
Or we sit at a table, with small tea carefully poured;
so we pass our time together, calm and delighted.

Emily Dickinson

I've known a Heaven, like a Tent—
To wrap its shining Yards—
Pluck up its stakes, and disappear—
Without the sound of Boards
Or Rip of Nail—Or Carpenter—
But just the miles of Stare—
That signalize a Show's Retreat—
In North America—

No Trace—no Figment of the Thing
That dazzled, Yesterday,
No Ring—no Marvel—
Men and Feats—
Dissolved as utterly—
As Bird's far Navigation
Discloses just a Hue—
A plash of Oars, a Gaiety—
Then swallowed up, of View.

Letter to N.Y.

Elizabeth Bishop

for Louise Crane

In your next letter I wish you'd say
where you are going and what you are doing;
how are the plays, and after the plays
what other pleasures you're pursuing:

taking cabs in the middle of the night,
driving as if to save your soul
where the road goes round and round the park
and the meter glares like a moral owl,

and the trees look so queer and green
standing alone in big black caves
and suddenly you're in a different place
where everything seems to happen in waves,

and most of the jokes you just can't catch,
like dirty words rubbed off a slate,
and the songs are loud but somehow dim
and it gets so terribly late,

and coming out of the brownstone house
to the gray sidewalk, the watered street,
one side of the buildings rises with the sun
like a glistening field of wheat.

—Wheat, not oats, dear. I'm afraid
if it's wheat it's none of your sowing,
nevertheless I'd like to know
what you are doing and where you are going.

Dilemma

David Budbill

I want to be
          famous
so I can be
          humble
about being
          famous.

What good is my
          humility
when I am
          stuck
in this
          obscurity?

from Song of Myself

Walt Whitman

Who goes there? hankering, gross, mystical, nude;
How is it I extract strength from the beef I eat?

What is a man anyhow? what am I? what are you?

All I mark as my own you shall offset it with your own,
Else it were time lost listening to me . . .

Why should I pray? why should I venerate and be
    ceremonious?
Having pried through the strata, analyzed to a hair,
    counsel'd with doctors and calculated close,
I find no sweeter fat than sticks to my own bones.

In all people I see myself, none more, and not one a barley-
    corn less,
And the good or bad I say of myself I say of them.

I know I am solid and sound,
To me the converging objects of the universe perpetually flow
All are written to me, and I must get what the writing means.

I know I am deathless,
I know this orbit of mine cannot be swept by a carpenter's
  compass,
I know I shall not pass like a child's carlacue cut with a
  burnt stick at night.

I know I am august,
I do not trouble my spirit to vindicate itself or be understood,
I see that the elementary laws never apologize,
(I reckon I behave no prouder than the level I plant my
  house by, after all.)

I exist as I am, that is enough,
If no other in the world be aware I sit content,
And if each and all be aware I sit content.

One world is aware and by far the largest to me, and that is
  myself,
And whether I come to my own to-day or in ten thousand
  or ten million years,
I can cheerfully take it now, or with equal cheerfulness I
  can wait.

New Yorkers

Edward Field

Everywhere else in the country, if someone asks,
How are you? you are required to answer,
like a phrase book, Fine, and you?

Only in New York can you say, Not so good, or even,
Rotten, and launch into your miseries and symptoms,
then yawn and look bored when they interrupt
to go into the usual endless detail about their own.

Nodding mechanically, you look at your watch.
Look, angel, I've got to run, I'm late for my . . . uh . . .
uh . . . analyst. But let's definitely
get together soon.

In just as sincere a voice as yours,
they come back with, Definitely!
and both of you know what that means,
Never.

Soaking Up Sun

Tom Hennen

Today there is the kind of sunshine old men love, the kind of day when my grandfather would sit on the south side of the wooden corncrib where the sunlight warmed slowly all through the day like a wood stove. One after another dry leaves fell. No painful memories came. Everything was lit by a halo of light. The cornstalks glinted bright as pieces of glass. From the fields and cottonwood grove came the damp smell of mushrooms, of things going back to earth. I sat with my grandfather then. Sheep came up to us as we sat there, their oily wool so warm to my fingers, like a strange and magic snow. My grandfather whittled sweet smelling apple sticks just to get at the scent. His thumb had a permanent groove in it where the back of the knife blade rested. He let me listen to the wind, the wild geese, the soft dialect of sheep, while his own silence taught me every secret thing he knew.

Late Hours

Lisel Mueller

On summer nights the world
moves within earshot
on the interstate with its swish
and growl, an occasional siren
that sends chills through us.
Sometimes, on clear, still nights,
voices float into our bedroom,
lunar and fragmented,
as if the sky had let them go
long before our birth.

In winter we close the windows
and read Chekhov,
nearly weeping for his world.

What luxury, to be so happy
that we can grieve
over imaginary lives.

3

MUSIC

Scrambled Eggs and Whiskey

Hayden Carruth

Scrambled eggs and whiskey
in the false-dawn light. Chicago,
a sweet town, bleak, God knows,
but sweet. Sometimes. And
weren't we fine tonight?
When Hank set up that limping
treble roll behind me
my horn just growled and I
thought my heart would burst.
And Brad M. pressing with the
soft stick and Joe-Anne
singing low. Here we are now
in the White Tower, leaning
on one another, too tired
to go home. But don't say a word,
don't tell a soul, they wouldn't
understand, they couldn't, never
in a million years, how fine,
how magnificent we were
in that old club tonight.

Mehitabel's Song

Don Marquis

there s a dance or two
in the old dame yet
believe me you
there s a dance or two
before i m through
you get me pet
there s a dance or two
in the old dame yet

life s too dam funny
for me to explain
it s kicks or money
life s too dam funny
it s one day sunny
the next day rain
life s too dam funny
for me to explain

but toujours gai
is my motto kid
the devil s to pay
but toujours gai
and once in a way
let s lift the lid
but toujours gai
is my motto kid

thank god i m a lady
and class will tell
you hear me sadie
thank god i m a lady
my past is shady
but wotthehell
thank god I m a lady
and class will tell

Nightclub

Billy Collins

You are so beautiful and I am a fool
to be in love with you
is a theme that keeps coming up
in songs and poems.
There seems to be no room for variation.
I have never heard anyone sing
I am so beautiful
and you are a fool to be in love with me,
even though this notion has surely
crossed the minds of women and men alike.
You are so beautiful, too bad you are a fool
is another one you don't hear.
Or, you are a fool to consider me beautiful.
That one you will never hear, guaranteed.

For no particular reason this afternoon
I am listening to Johnny Hartman
whose dark voice can curl around
the concepts of love, beauty, and foolishness
like no one else's can.
It feels like smoke curling up from a cigarette
someone left burning on a baby grand piano
around three o'clock in the morning;
smoke that billows up into the bright lights
while out there in the darkness
some of the beautiful fools have gathered

around little tables to listen,
some with their eyes closed,
others leaning forward into the music
as if it were holding them up,
or twirling the loose ice in a glass,
slipping by degrees into a rhythmic dream.

Yes, there is all this foolish beauty,
borne beyond midnight,
that has no desire to go home,
especially now when everyone in the room
is watching the large man with the tenor sax
that hangs from his neck like a golden fish.
He moves forward to the edge of the stage
and hands the instrument down to me
and nods that I should play.
So I put the mouthpiece to my lips
and blow into it with all my living breath.
We are all so foolish,
my long bebop solo begins by saying,
so damn foolish
we have become beautiful without even knowing it.

Alley Violinist

Robert Lax

if you were an alley violinist

and they threw you money
from three windows

and the first note contained
a nickel and said:
when you play, we dance and
sing, signed
a very poor family

and the second one contained
a dime and said:
i like your playing very much,
signed
a sick old lady

and the last one contained
a dollar and said:
beat it,

would you:
stand there and play?

beat it?

walk away playing your fiddle?

Cradle Song

Jim Schley

Reapers and sowers, gleaners and drovers:
All go to sleep.
Plowers and fleecers: twelve o'clock mowers:
Go to sleep, to sleep.

As far, as far as we know.
As far as we know.

Elephant trainers: wallpaper hangers: corncob pipe-smoking porters:
Will all at the wave of a hat go to sleep.
Maplesap boilers: climbing rope coilers:
To sleep, before long—or gradually, to sleep.
Congressional pages: pundits and sages: acolytes and choir girls:
To sleep now, to sleep.

As far as we know.
As far as we know, we'll know.

Shopkeepers, goalkeepers, timekeepers, lighthouse-keepers:
At long last, to sleep.
Steeplejacks, lumberjacks, jack-hammerers, and apple-jacks:
To sleep, now—to sleep.

As far as we know, when we know;
as far as we know.

Deep as the chimney shaft
That passes your bed,
And wide as the rough black roof overhead:
Now to sleep, tiny child, now to sleep.

As far as we know.
As far as we know.

Her Door

Mary Leader

for my daughter Sara Marie

There was a time her door was never closed.
Her music box played "Für Elise" in plinks.
Her crib new-bought—I drew her sleeping there.

The little drawing sits beside my chair.
These days, she ornaments her hands with rings.
She's seventeen. Her door is one I knock.

There was a time I daily brushed her hair
By window light—I bathed her, in the sink
In sunny water, in the kitchen, there.

I've bought her several thousand things to wear,
And now this boy buys her silver rings.
He goes inside her room and shuts the door.

Those days, to rock her was a form of prayer.
She'd gaze at me, and blink, and I would sing
Of bees and horses, in the pasture, there.

The drawing sits as still as nap-time air—
Her curled-up hand—that precious line, her cheek . . .
Next year her door will stand, again, ajar
But she herself will not be living there.

The Pupil

Donald Justice

Picture me, the shy pupil at the door,
One small, tight fist clutching the dread Czerny.
Back then time was still harmony, not money,
And I could spend a whole week practicing for
That moment on the threshold.
                                   Then to take courage,
And enter, and pass among mysterious scents,
And sit quite straight, and with a frail confidence
Assault the keyboard with a childish flourish!

Only to lose my place, or forget the key,
And almost doubt the very metronome
(Outside, the traffic, the laborers going home),
And still to bear on across Chopin or Brahms,
Stupid and wild with love equally for the storms
Of C# minor and the calms of C.

Piano

D. H. Lawrence

Softly, in the dusk, a woman is singing to me;
Taking me back down the vista of years, till I see
A child sitting under the piano, in the boom of the tingling strings
And pressing the small, poised feet of a mother who smiles as she
    sings.

In spite of myself, the insidious mastery of song
Betrays me back, till the heart of me weeps to belong
To the old Sunday evenings at home, with winter outside
And hymns in the cosy parlour, the tinkling piano our guide.

So now it is vain for the singer to burst into clamour
With the great black piano appassionato. The glamour
Of childish days is upon me, my manhood is cast
Down in the flood of remembrance, I weep like a child for the past.

Instrument of Choice

Robert Phillips

She was a girl
no one ever chose
for teams or clubs,
dances or dates,

so she chose the instrument
no one else wanted:
the tuba. Big as herself,
heavy as her heart,

its golden tubes
and coils encircled her
like a lover's embrace.
Its body pressed on hers.

Into its mouthpiece she blew
life, its deep-throated
oompahs, oompahs sounding,
almost, like mating cries.

Homage: Doo-Wop

Joseph Stroud

There's so little sweetness in the music I hear now,
no croons, no doo-wop or slow ones where you could
hug up with someone and hold them against your body,
feel their heart against yours, touch their cheek
with your cheek—and it was OK, it was allowed,
even the mothers standing around at the birthday party,
the rug rolled back in the living room, didn't mind
if you held their daughters as you swayed to the music,
eyes squeezed shut, holding each other, and holding on
to the song, until you almost stopped moving,
just shuffled there, embracing, as the Moonglows
and Penguins crooned, and the mothers looked on
not with disapproval or scorn, looked on with their eyes
dreaming, as if looking from a thousand miles away, as if
from over the mountain and across the sea, a look
on their faces I didn't understand, not knowing then
those other songs I would someday enter, not knowing
how I would shimmer and writhe, jig like a puppet
doing the *shimmy-shimmy-kokobop*, or glide from turn
to counterturn within the waltz, not knowing
how I would hold the other through the night
and across the years, holding on for love and dear life,
for solace and kindness, learning the dance as we go,
learning from those first, awkward, shuffling steps,
that sweetness and doo-wop back at the beginning.

The Persistence of Song

Howard Moss

Although it is not yet evening,
The secretaries have changed their frocks
As if it were time for dancing,
And locked up in the scholars' books
There is a kind of rejoicing,
There is a kind of singing
That even the dark stone canyon makes
As though all fountains were going
At once, and the color flowed from bricks
In one wild, lit upsurging.

What is the weather doing?
And who arrived on a scallop shell
With the smell of the sea this morning?
—Creating a small upheaval
High above the scaffolding
By saying, "All will be well.
There is a kind of rejoicing."

Is there a kind of rejoicing
In saying, "All will be well?"
High above the scaffolding,
Creating a small upheaval,
The smell of the sea this morning
Arrived on a scallop shell.
What was the weather doing

In one wild, lit upsurging?
At once, the color flowed from bricks
As though all fountains were going,
And even the dark stone canyon makes
Here a kind of singing,
And there a kind of rejoicing,
And locked up in the scholars' books
There is a time for dancing
When the secretaries have changed their frocks,
And though it is not yet evening,

There is the persistence of song.

Ooly Pop a Cow

David Huddle

for Bess and Molly

My brother Charles
brought home the news
the kids were saying
take a flying leap
and eat me raw
and be bop a lula.

Forty miles he rode
the bus there and back.
The dog and I met him
at the door, panting
for hoke poke, hoke
de waddy waddy hoke poke.

In Cu Chi, Vietnam,
I heard tapes somebody's
sister sent of wild thing,
I think I love you
and hey now, what's that
sound, everybody look what's . . .

Now it's my daughters
bringing home no-duh,
rock out, whatever,
like I totally
paused, and like
I'm like . . .

I'm like Mother, her hands
in biscuit dough,
her ears turning red
from ain' nothin butta,
blue monday, and
tutti frutti, aw rooty!

Elevator Music

Henry Taylor

A tune with no more substance than the air,
performed on underwater instruments,
is proper to this short lift from the earth.
It hovers as we draw into ourselves
and turn our reverent eyes toward the lights
that count us to our various destinies.
We're all in this together, the song says,
and later we'll descend. The melody
is like a name we don't recall just now
that still keeps on insisting it is there.

The Grain of Sound

Robert Morgan

A banjo maker in the mountains,
when looking out for wood to carve
an instrument, will walk among
the trees and knock on trunks. He'll hit
the bark and listen for a note.
A hickory makes the brightest sound;
the poplar has a mellow ease.
But only straightest grain will keep
the purity of tone, the sought-
for depth that makes the licks sparkle.
A banjo has a shining shiver.
Its twangs will glitter like the light
on splashing water, even though
its face is just a drum of hide
of cow, or cat, or even skunk.
The hide will magnify the note,
the sad of honest pain, the chill
blood-song, lament, confession, haunt,
as tree will sing again from root
and vein and sap and twig in wind
and cat will moan as hand plucks nerve,
picks bone and skin and gut and pricks
the heart as blood will answer blood
and love begins to knock along the grain.

I Will Make You Brooches

Robert Louis Stevenson

I will make you brooches and toys for your delight
Of bird-song at morning and star-shine at night.
I will make a palace fit for you and me
Of green days in forests and blue days at sea.

I will make my kitchen, and you shall keep your room,
Where white flows the river and bright blows the broom,
And you shall wash your linen and keep your body white
In rainfall at morning and dewfall at night.

And this shall be for music when no one else is near,
The fine song for singing, the rare song to hear!
That only I remember, that only you admire,
Of the broad road that stretches and the roadside fire.

The Dance

C. K. Williams

A middle-aged woman, quite plain, to be polite about it, and
    somewhat stout, to be more courteous still,
but when she and the rather good-looking, much younger man
    she's with get up to dance,
her forearm descends with such delicate lightness, such restrained
    but confident ardor athwart his shoulder,
drawing him to her with such a firm, compelling warmth, and
    moving him with effortless grace
into the union she's instantly established with the not at all
    rhythmically solid music in this second-rate café,

that something in the rest of us, some doubt about ourselves, some
    sad conjecture, seems to be allayed,
nothing that we'd ever thought of as a real lack, nothing not to be
    admired or be repentant for,
but something to which we've never adequately given credence,
which might have consoling implications about how we misbe-
    lieve ourselves, and so the world,
that world beyond us which so often disappoints, but which
    sometimes shows us, lovely, what we are.

The Investment

Robert Frost

Over back where they speak of life as staying
("You couldn't call it living, for it ain't"),
There was an old, old house renewed with paint,
And in it a piano loudly playing.

Out in the plowed ground in the cold a digger,
Among unearthed potatoes standing still,
Was counting winter dinners, one a hill,
With half an ear to the piano's vigor.

All that piano and new paint back there,
Was it some money suddenly come into?
Or some extravagance young love had been to?
Or old love on an impulse not to care—

Not to sink under being man and wife,
But get some color and music out of life?

The Dumka

B. H. Fairchild

His parents would sit alone together
on the blue divan in the small living room
listening to Dvorak's piano quintet.
They would sit there in their old age,
side by side, quite still, backs rigid, hands
in their laps, and look straight ahead
at the yellow light of the phonograph
that seemed as distant as a lamplit
window seen across the plains late at night.
They would sit quietly as something dense

and radiant swirled around them, something
like the dust storms of the thirties that began
by smearing the sky green with doom
but afterwards drenched the air with an amber
glow and then vanished, leaving profiles
of children on pillows and a pale gauze
over mantles and table tops. But it was
the memory of dust that encircled them now
and made them smile faintly and raise
or bow their heads as they spoke about

the farm in twilight with piano music
spiraling out across red roads and fields
of maize, bread lines in the city, women
and men lining main street like mannequins,

and then the war, the white frame rent house,
and the homecoming, the homecoming,
the homecoming, and afterwards, green lawns
and a new piano with its mahogany gleam
like pond ice at dawn, and now alone
in the house in the vanishing neighborhood,

the slow mornings of coffee and newspapers
and evenings of music and scattered bits
of talk like leaves suddenly fallen before
one notices the new season. And they would sit
there alone and soon he would reach across
and lift her hand as if it were the last unbroken
leaf and he would hold her hand in his hand
for a long time and they would look far off
into the music of their lives as they sat alone
together in the room in the house in Kansas.

Lawrence Ferlinghetti

The Green Street Mortuary Marching Band
        marches right down Green Street
                and turns into Columbus Avenue
                      where all the café sitters at
                            the sidewalk café tables
                                sit talking and laughing and
                                  looking right through it
as if it happened every day in
  little old wooden North Beach San Francisco
      but at the same time feeling thrilled
          by the stirring sound of the gallant marching band
             as if it were celebrating life and
                             never heard of death

And right behind it comes the open hearse
  with the closed casket and the
          big framed picture under glass propped up
        showing the patriarch who
                      has just croaked
And now all seven members of
  the Green Street Mortuary Marching Band
    with the faded gold braid on their
                  beat-up captains' hats
      raise their bent axes and
        start blowing all more or less
                    together and

out comes this Onward Christian Soldiers like
you heard it once upon a time only
much slower with a dead beat

And now you see all the relatives behind the
closed glass windows of the long black cars and
their faces are all shiny like they
been weeping with washcloths and
all super serious
like as if the bottom has just dropped out of
their private markets and
there's the widow all in weeds, and the sister with the
bent frame and the mad brother who never got through school
and Uncle Louie with the wig and there they all are assembled
together and facing each other maybe for the first time in a long
time but their masks and public faces are all in place as they face
outward behind the traveling corpse up ahead and oompah oompah goes the band very slow with the trombones and the tuba
and the trumpets and the big bass drum and the corpse hears
nothing or everything and it's a glorious autumn day in old
North Beach if only he could have lived to see it Only we
wouldn't have had the band who half an hour later can be seen
straggling back silent along the sidewalks looking like hungover
brokendown Irish bartenders dying for a drink or a last hurrah

4

SCENES

Poem to Be Read at 3 A.M.

Donald Justice

Excepting the diner
On the outskirts
The town of Ladora
At 3 A.M.
Was dark but
For my headlights
And up in
One second-story room
A single light
Where someone
Was sick or
Perhaps reading
As I drove past
At seventy
Not thinking
This poem
Is for whoever
Had the light on

The Swimming Pool

Thomas Lux

All around the apt. swimming pool
the boys stare at the girls
and the girls look everywhere but the opposite
or down or up. It is
as it was a thousand years ago: the fat
boy has it hardest, he
takes the sneers,
prefers the winter so he can wear
his heavy pants and sweater.
Today, he's here with the others.
Better they are cruel to him in his presence
than out. Of the five here now (three boys,
two girls) one is fat, three cruel,
and one, a girl, wavers to the side,
all the world tearing at her.
As yet she has no breasts
(her friend does) and were it not
for the forlorn fat boy whom she joins
in taunting, she could not bear her terror,
which is the terror
of being him. Does it make her happy
that she has no need, right now, of ingratiation,
of acting fool to salve
her loneliness? She doesn't seem
so happy. She is like
the lower middle class, that fatal group

handed crumbs so they can drop a few
down lower, to the poor, so they won't kill
the rich. All around
the apt. swimming pool
there is what's everywhere: forsakenness
and fear, a disdain for those beneath us
rather than a rage
against the ones above: the exploiters,
the oblivious and unabashedly cruel.

Dostoevsky

Charles Bukowski

against the wall, the firing squad ready.
then he got a reprieve.
suppose they had shot Dostoevsky?
before he wrote all that?
I suppose it wouldn't have
mattered
not directly.
there are billions of people who have
never read him and never
will.
but as a young man I know that he
got me through the factories,
past the whores,
lifted me high through the night
and put me down
in a better
place.
even while in the bar
drinking with the other
derelicts,
I was glad they gave Dostoevsky a
reprieve,
it gave me one,
allowed me to look directly at those
rancid faces
in my world,

death pointing its finger,
I held fast,
an immaculate drunk
sharing the stinking dark with
my
brothers.

After a Movie

Henry Taylor

The last small credits fade
as house lights rise. Dazed in that radiant instant
of transition, you dwindle through the lobby
and out to curbside, pulling on a glove
with the decisive competence
of the scarred detective

or his quarry. Scanning
the rainlit street for taxicabs, you visualize,
without looking, your image in the window
of the jeweler's shop, where white hands hover
above the string of luminous pearls
on a faceless velvet bust.

Someone across the street
enters a bar, leaving behind a charged vacancy
in which you cut to the dim booth inside,
where you are seated, glancing at the door.
You lift an eyebrow, recognizing
the unnamed colleague

who will conspire with you
against whatever the volatile script provides. . . .
A cab pulls up. You stoop into the dark
and settle toward a version of yourself.

Your profile cruises past the city
on a home-drifting stream

through whose surface, sometimes,
you glimpse the life between the streambed and the ripples,
as, when your gestures are your own again,
your fingers lift a cup beyond whose rim
a room bursts into clarity
and light falls on all things.

Summer Storm

Dana Gioia

We stood on the rented patio
While the party went on inside.
You knew the groom from college.
I was a friend of the bride.

We hugged the brownstone wall behind us
To keep our dress clothes dry
And watched the sudden summer storm
Floodlit against the sky.

The rain was like a waterfall
Of brilliant beaded light,
Cool and silent as the stars
The storm hid from the night.

To my surprise, you took my arm—
A gesture you didn't explain—
And we spoke in whispers, as if we two
Might imitate the rain.

Then suddenly the storm receded
As swiftly as it came.
The doors behind us opened up.
The hostess called your name.

I watched you merge into the group,
Aloof and yet polite.
We didn't speak another word
Except to say goodnight.

Why does that evening's memory
Return with this night's storm—
A party twenty years ago,
Its disappointments warm?

There are so many *might have beens*,
What ifs that won't stay buried,
Other cities, other jobs,
Strangers we might have married.

And memory insists on pining
For places it never went,
As if life would be happier
Just by being different.

Woolworth's

Mark Irwin

for Gerald Stern

Everything stands wondrously multicolored
and at attention in the always Christmas air.
What scent lingers unrecognizably
between that of popcorn, grilled cheese sandwiches,

malted milkballs, and parakeets? Maybe you came here
in winter to buy your daughter a hamster
and were detained by the bin

of *Multicolored Thongs*, four pair
for a dollar. Maybe you came here to buy
some envelopes, the light blue *par avion* ones

with airplanes, but caught yourself, lost,
daydreaming, saying *it's too late* over the glassy
diorama of cakes and pies. Maybe you came here

to buy a lampshade, the fake crimped
kind, and suddenly you remember
your grandmother, dead

twenty years, floating through the old
house like a curtain. Maybe you're retired,
on Social Security, and came here for the *Roast*

Turkey Dinner, or the *Liver and Onions,*
or just to stare into a black circle
of coffee and to get warm. Or maybe

the big church down the street is closed
now during the day, and you're homeless and poor,
or you're rich, or it doesn't matter what you are

with a little loose change jangling in your pocket,
begging to be spent, because you wandered in
and somewhere between the bin of animal crackers

and the little zoo in the back of the store
you lost something, and because you came here
not to forget, but to remember to live.

Worked Late on a Tuesday Night

Deborah Garrison

Again.
Midtown is blasted out and silent,
drained of the crowd and its doggy day.
I trample the scraps of deli lunches
some ate outdoors as they stared dumbly
or hooted at us career girls—the haggard
beauties, the vivid can-dos, open raincoats aflap
in the March wind as we crossed to and fro
in front of the Public Library.

Never thought you'd be one of them,
did you, little lady?
Little Miss Phi Beta Kappa,
with your closetful of pleated
skirts, twenty-nine till death do us
part! Don't you see?
The good schoolgirl turns thirty,
forty, singing the song of time management
all day long, lugging the briefcase

home. So at 10:00 PM
you're standing here
with your hand in the air,
cold but too stubborn to reach
into your pocket for a glove, cursing
the freezing rain as though it were

your difficulty. It's pathetic,
and nobody's fault but
your own. Now

the tears,
down into the collar.
Cabs, cabs, but none for hire.
I haven't had dinner; I'm not half
of what I meant to be.
Among other things, the mother
of three. Too tired, tonight,
to seduce the father.

The Farmhouse

Reed Whittemore

Our house is an old farmhouse, whose properties
The town has gradually purchased, leaving it
Only a city lot and a few trees
Of all that wood and busheldom and breeze
It once served. It is high and square,
And its lines, such as they are, have been muddled by several
Conflicting remodelers, whose care
In widening, lengthening, adding on, letting in air
Has left it with four kinds of windows, three porches
And a door that leads to a closet that is not there.

The city houses around us have borrowed from verse
And the Old Dominion; their cosmopolitan
Muddle is elegant next to ours.
We think of moving, and say we'll add no more dollars
To those already spent making a box
Of what was, is and will be, forever, a box,
When there's land, empty and unboxed, down a few blocks
Waiting.
We say this as we pull down, pull up, push out
And generally persevere with our renovating—

That is, making new again—knowing
That houses like our house are not made new again
Any more than a man is. All that growing
Up and away from the land, that bowing

To impersonal social forces that transform
Wheat fields into rows of two-bedroom ramblers
Must be acknowledged; but the warm
Part of our country boy will not conform.
It remains, behind new windows, doors and porches,
Hugging its childhood, staying down on the farm.

wrist-wrestling father

Orval Lund

For my father

On the maple wood we placed our elbows
and gripped hands, the object to bend
the other's arm to the kitchen table.
We flexed our arms and waited for the sign.

I once shot a wild goose.
I once stood not twenty feet from a buck deer unnoticed.
I've seen a woods full of pink lady slippers.
I once caught a 19-inch trout on a tiny fly.
I've seen the Pacific, I've seen the Atlantic,
I've watched whales in each.

I once heard Lenny Bruce tell jokes.
I've seen Sandy Koufax pitch a baseball.
I've heard Paul Desmond play the saxophone.
I've been to London to see the Queen.
I've had dinner with a Nobel Prize poet.

I wrote a poem once with every word but one just right.
I've fathered two fine sons
and loved the same woman for twenty-five years.

But I've never been more amazed
than when I snapped my father's arm down to the table.

Yorkshiremen in Pub Gardens

Gavin Ewart

As they sit there, happily drinking,
their strokes, cancers and so forth are not in their minds.
    Indeed, what earthly good would thinking
about the future (which is Death) do? Each summer finds
      beer in their hands in big pint glasses.
      And so their leisure passes.

Perhaps the older ones allow some inkling
into their thoughts. Being hauled, as a kid, upstairs to bed
    screaming for a teddy or a tinkling
musical box, against their will. Each Joe or Fred
      wants longer with the life and lasses.
      And so their time passes.

Second childhood; and 'Come in, number eighty!'
shouts inexorably the man in charge of the boating pool.
    When you're called you must go, matey,
so don't complain, keep it all calm and cool,
      there's masses of time yet, masses, masses . . .
      And so their life passes.

Noah

Roy Daniells

They gathered around and told him not to do it,
They formed a committee and tried to take control,
They cancelled his building permit and they stole
His plans. I sometimes wonder he got through it.
He told them wrath was coming, they would rue it,
He begged them to believe the tides would roll,
He offered them passage to his destined goal,
A new world. They were finished and he knew it.
All to no end.
          And then the rain began.
A spatter at first that barely wet the soil,
Then showers, quick rivulets lacing the town,
Then deluge universal. The old man
Arthritic from his years of scorn and toil
Leaned from the admiral's walk and watched them drown.

5

LOVERS

A Red, Red Rose

Robert Burns

O my luve's like a red, red rose,
    That's newly sprung in June;
O my luve's like the melodie
    That's sweetly played in tune.

As fair art thou, my bonnie lass,
    So deep in luve am I;
And I will luve thee still, my dear,
    Till a' the seas gang dry.

Till a' the seas gang dry, my dear,
    And the rocks melt wi' the sun:
O I will luve thee still, my dear,
    When the sands o' life shall run.

And fare thee weel, my only luve,
    And fare thee weel awhile!
And I will come again, my luve,
    Though it were ten thousand mile.

When I Heard at the Close of Day

Walt Whitman

When I heard at the close of the day how my name had been
   receiv'd with plaudits in the capitol, still it was not a happy
   night for me that follow'd,
And else, when I carous'd, or when my plans were accomplish'd,
   still I was not happy,
But the day when I rose at dawn from the bed of perfect health,
   refresh'd, singing, inhaling the ripe breath of autumn,
When I saw the full moon in the west grow pale and disappear in
   the morning light,
When I wander'd alone over the beach, and undressing bathed,
   laughing with the cool waters, and saw the sun rise,
And when I thought how my dear friend my lover was on his way
   coming, O then I was happy,
O then each breath tasted sweeter, and all that day my food
   nourish'd me more, and the beautiful day pass'd well,
And the next came with equal joy, and with the next at evening
   came my friend,
And that night while all was still I heard the waters roll slowly
   continually up the shores,
I heard the hissing rustle of the liquid and sands as directed to me
   whispering to congratulate me,
For the one I love most lay sleeping by me under the same cover in
   the cool night,
In the stillness in the autumn moonbeams his face was inclined
   toward me,
And his arm lay lightly around my breast—and that night I was
   happy.

First Love

John Clare

I ne'er was struck before that hour
    With love so sudden and so sweet.
Her face it bloomed like a sweet flower
    And stole my heart away complete.
My face turned pale as deadly pale,
    My legs refused to walk away,
And when she looked "what could I ail?"
    My life and all seemed turned to clay.

And then my blood rushed to my face
    And took my sight away.
The trees and bushes round the place
    Seemed midnight at noonday.
I could not see a single thing,
    Words from my eyes did start;
They spoke as chords do from the string
    And blood burnt round my heart.

Are flowers the winter's choice?
    Is love's bed always snow?
She seemed to hear my silent voice
    And love's appeal to know.
I never saw so sweet a face
    As that I stood before:
My heart has left its dwelling-place
    And can return no more.

He Wishes for the Cloths of Heaven

W. B. Yeats

Had I the heavens' embroidered cloths,
Enwrought with golden and silver light,
The blue and the dim and the dark cloths
Of night and light and the half-light,
I would spread the cloths under your feet:
But I, being poor, have only my dreams;
I have spread my dreams under your feet;
Tread softly because you tread on my dreams.

Sonnet

C. B. Trail

This is for the afternoon we lay in the leaves
After it had been winter for half a year,
And I kissed you and unbuttoned your jeans
And touched you and made you smile, my dear.
And of all the good things that love means,
One of them is to touch you there
And make you smile, among the leaves,
And feel your wetness and your sweet short hair,
And kiss your breasts and put my tongue
Into the delirium between your soft pale thighs,
Because the winter has been much too long
And soon will come again, when this love dies.
>   I will hear sermons preached, and some of them be true,
>   But I will not regret that afternoon with you.

Politics

W. B. Yeats

*"In our time the destiny of man presents its
meanings in political terms"*
—THOMAS MANN

How can I, that girl standing there,
My attention fix
On Roman or on Russian
Or on Spanish politics,
Yet here's a travelled man that knows
What he talks about,
And there's a politician
That has both read and thought,
And maybe what they say is true
Of war and war's alarms,
But O that I were young again
And held her in my arms.

23 May 1938

Magellan Street, 1974

Maxine Kumin

This is the year you fall in
love with the Bengali poet,
and the Armenian bakery stays open
Saturday nights until eleven
across the street from your sunny
apartment with steep fo'c'sle stairs
up to an attic bedroom.
Three-decker tenements flank you.
Cyclone fences enclose
flamingos on diaper-size lawns.

This is the year, in a kitchen
you brighten with pots of basil
and untidy mint, I see how
your life will open, will burst from
the maze in its walled-in garden
and streak toward the horizon.
Your pastel maps lie open
on the counter as we stand here
not quite up to exchanging
our lists of sorrows, our day books,
our night thoughts, and burn the first batch
of chocolate walnut cookies.

Of course you move on,
my circumnavigator.
Tonight as I cruise past your corner,
a light goes on in the window.
Two shapes sit at a table.

Animals

Frank O'Hara

Have you forgotten what we were like then
when we were still first rate
and the day came fat with an apple in its mouth

it's no use worrying about Time
but we did have a few tricks up our sleeves
and turned some sharp corners

the whole pasture looked like our meal
we didn't need speedometers
we could manage cocktails out of ice and water

I wouldn't want to be faster
or greener than now if you were with me O you
were the best of all my days

Lending Out Books

Hal Sirowitz

You're always giving, my therapist said.
You have to learn how to take. Whenever
you meet a woman, the first thing you do
is lend her your books. You think she'll
have to see you again in order to return them.
But what happens is, she doesn't have the time
to read them, & she's afraid if she sees you again
you'll expect her to talk about them, & will
want to lend her even more. So she
cancels the date. You end up losing
a lot of books. You should borrow hers.

The Changed Man

Robert Phillips

If you were to hear me imitating Pavarotti
in the shower every morning, you would know
how much you have changed my life.

If you were to see me stride across the park,
waving to strangers, then you would know
I am a changed man—like Scrooge

awakened from his bad dreams feeling feather-
light, angel-happy, laughing the father
of a long line of bright laughs—

"It is still not too late to change my life!"
It is changed. Me, who felt short-changed.
Because of you I no longer hate my body.

Because of you I buy new clothes.
Because of you I'm a warrior of joy.
Because of you and me. Drop by

this Saturday morning and discover me
fiercely pulling weeds gladly, dedicated
as a born-again gardener.

Drop by on Sunday—I'll Turtlewax
your sky-blue sports car, no sweat. I'll greet
enemies with a handshake, forgive debtors

with a papal largesse. It's all because
of you. Because of you and me,
I've become one changed man.

The Constant North

J. F. Hendry

Encompass me, my lover,
With your eyes' wide calm.
Though noonday shadows are assembling doom,
The sun remains when I remember them;
And death, if it should come,
Must fall like quiet snow from such clear skies.

Minutes we snatched from the unkind winds
Are grown into daffodils by the sea's
Edge, mocking its green miseries;
Yet I seek you hourly still, over
A new Atlantis loneliness, blind
As a restless needle held by the constant north we
    always have in mind.

On the Strength of All Conviction
and the Stamina of Love

Jennifer Michael Hecht

Sometimes I think
we could have gone on.
All of us. Trying. Forever.

But they didn't fill
the desert with pyramids.
They just built some. Some.

They're not still out there,
building them now. Everyone,
everywhere, gets up, and goes home.

Yet we must not
Diabolize time. Right?
We must not curse the passage of time.

The Loft

Richard Jones

I lay on her bed
while she opened windows
so we could see the river
and the factories beyond.
Afternoon light falling
beautifully into the room,
she burned candles,
incense, talking quietly
as I listened—
I, who conspired
to make this happen,
weaving a web of words that held
this moment at its center.
What could I say now?
That I am a man
empty of desire?
She stood beside the bed,
looking down at me
as if she were dreaming,
as if I were a dream,
as if she too had come
to the final shore of longing.
I lay, calm as a lake
reflecting the nothingness
of late summer sky.

Then she spoke—
she said my name—
and I, who did not love her,
opened my arms.

This Is Just to Say

William Carlos Williams

I have eaten
the plums
that were in
the icebox

and which
you were probably
saving
for breakfast

Forgive me
they were delicious
so sweet
and so cold

This Is Just to Say

Erica-Lynn Gambino

(for William Carlos Williams)

I have just
asked you to
get out of my
apartment

even though
you never
thought
I would

Forgive me
you were
driving
me insane

Venetian Air

Thomas Moore

Row gently here, my gondolier; so softly wake the tide,
That not an ear on earth may hear, but hers to whom we glide.
Had Heaven but tongues to speak, as well as starry eyes to see,
Oh! think what tales 'twould have to tell of wandering youths
    like me!

Now rest thee here, my gondolier; hush, hush, for up I go,
To climb yon light balcony's height, while thou keep'st watch
    below.
Ah! did we take for Heaven above but half such pains as we
Take day and night for woman's love, what angels we should
    be!

Summer Morning

Louis Simpson

There are whole blocks in New York
Where no one lives—
A district of small factories.
And there's a hotel; one morning

When I was there with a girl
We saw in the window opposite
Men and women working at their machines.
Now and then one looked up.

Toys, hardware—whatever their made,
It's been worn out.
I'm fifteen years older myself—
Bad years and good.

So I have spoiled my chances.
For what? Sheer laziness,
The thrill of an assignation,
My life that I hold in secret.

Comin thro' the Rye

Robert Burns

Comin thro' the rye, poor body,
Comin thro' the rye,
She draigl't a' her petticoatie
Comin thro' the rye.
Oh Jenny's a' weet poor body
Jenny's seldom dry;
She draigl't a' her petticoatie
Comin thro' the rye.

Gin a body meet a body,
Comin thro' the rye,
Gin a body kiss a body,
Need a body cry.
Oh Jenny's a' weet, poor body,
Jenny's seldom dry;
She draigl't a' her petticoatie
Comin thro' the rye.

Gin a body meet a body
Comin thro' the glen,
Gin a body kiss a body,
Need the warld ken!
Oh Jenny's a' weet, poor body,
Jenny's seldom dry;
She draigl't a' her petticoatie
Comin thro' the rye.

Topography

Sharon Olds

After we flew across the country we
got in bed, laid our bodies
delicately together, like maps laid
face to face, East to West, my
San Francisco against your New York, your
Fire Island against my Sonoma, my
New Orleans deep in your Texas, your Idaho
bright on my Great Lakes, my Kansas
burning against your Kansas your Kansas
burning against my Kansas, your Eastern
Standard Time pressing into my
Pacific Time, my Mountain Time
beating against your Central Time, your
sun rising swiftly from the right my
sun rising swiftly from the left your
moon rising slowly from the left my
moon rising slowly from the right until
all four bodies of the sky
burn above us, sealing us together,
all our cities twin cities,
all our states united, one
nation, indivisible, with liberty and justice for all.

Saturday Morning

Hugo Williams

Everyone who made love the night before
was walking around with flashing red lights
on top of their heads—a white-haired old gentleman,
a red-faced schoolboy, a pregnant woman
who smiled at me from across the street
and gave a little secret shrug,
as if the flashing red light on her head
was a small price to pay for what she knew.

Flight

Louis Jenkins

Past mishaps might be attributed to an incomplete understanding of the laws of aerodynamics or perhaps even to a more basic failure of the imagination, but were to be expected. Remember, this is solo flight unencumbered by bicycle parts, aluminum and nylon or even feathers. A *tour de force*, really. There's a lot of running and flapping involved and as you get older and heavier, a lot more huffing and puffing. But on a bright day like today with a strong headwind blowing up from the sea, when, having slipped the surly bonds of common sense and knowing she is watching, waiting in breathless anticipation, you send yourself hurtling down the long, green slope to the cliffs, who knows? You might just make it.

At Twenty-Three Weeks She Can No Longer See Anything South of Her Belly

Thom Ward

I'm painting my wife's toes
in Revlon Super Color Forty Nine.

I've no idea what I'm doing.
She asked me to get the bottle,

then crashed on our bed,
muscle-sore, pelvis-aching.

Lifting the brush, I skim
the excess polish across the glass,

daub a smidgen on her nail,
push it out in streaks

over the perfect surface
to the cuticle's edge.

I'm painting my wife's toes.
I've no idea what I'm doing.

The smell of fresh enamel
intoxicates. Each nail I glaze

is a tulip, a lobster,
a scarlet room where women

sit and talk, their sleek,
tinctured fingers sparking the air.

For the Life of Him and Her

Reed Whittemore

For the life of her she couldn't decide what to wear to the
    party.
All those clothes in the closet and not a thing to wear.
Nothing to wear, nothing wearable to a party,
Nothing at all in the closet for a girl to wear.

For the life of him he couldn't imagine what she was doing
    up there.
She had been messing around in that closet for at least an
    hour,
Trying on this, trying on that, trying on all those clothes
    up there,
So that they were already late for the party by at least an
    hour.

If only he wouldn't stand around down in the hall,
She could get herself dressed for the party, she knew she
    could somehow,
But he made her so nervous, he was just so nervous there in the
    hall
That she didn't think they would get to the party anyhow.

He didn't want to go to the party anyhow,
And he didn't want to stand and stand in the hall,
But he didn't want to tell her that he didn't want to go anyhow.
He just didn't want to, that's all.

Romantics

Johannes Brahms and Clara Schumann

Lisel Mueller

The modern biographers worry
"how far it went," their tender friendship.
They wonder just what it means
when he writes he thinks of her constantly,
his guardian angel, beloved friend.
The modern biographers ask
the rude, irrelevant question
of our age, as if the event
of two bodies meshing together
establishes the degree of love,
forgetting how softly Eros walked
in the nineteenth century, how a hand
held overlong or a gaze anchored
in someone's eyes could unseat a heart,
and nuances of address not known
in our egalitarian language
could make the redolent air
tremble and shimmer with the heat
of possibility. Each time I hear
the Intermezzi, sad
and lavish in their tenderness,
I imagine the two of them
sitting in a garden

among late-blooming roses
and dark cascades of leaves,
letting the landscape speak for them,
leaving us nothing to overhear.

Down in the Valley

Anonymous

Down in the valley, valley so low,
Hang your head over, hear the wind blow.
   Hear the wind blow, love, hear the wind blow,
   Hang your head over, hear the wind blow.

If you don't love me, love whom you please,
But throw your arms round me, give my heart ease.
   Give my heart ease, dear, give my heart ease.
   Throw your arms round me, give my heart ease.

Down in the valley, walking between,
Telling our story, here's what it sings:
   Here's what it sings, dear, here's what it sings,
   Telling our story, here's what it sings:

Roses of sunshine, vi'lets of dew,
Angels in heaven know I love you,
   Know I love you, dear, know I love you,
   Angels in heaven know I love you.

Build me a castle forty feet high,
So I can see her as she goes by,
   As she goes by, dear, as she goes by,
   So I can see her as she goes by.

Bird in a cage, love, bird in a cage,
Dying for freedom, ever a slave;
      Ever a slave, dear, ever a slave,
      Dying for freedom, ever a slave.

Write me a letter, send it by mail,
Send it in care of the Birmingham jail.
      Birmingham jail, love, Birmingham jail,
      Send it in care of the Birmingham jail.

The Middle Years

Walter McDonald

These are the nights we dreamed of,
snow drifting over a cabin roof
in the mountains, enough stacked wood
and meat to last a week, alone at last

in a rented A-frame, isolated,
without power, high in the San Juan.
Our children are safe as they'll ever be
seeking their fortune in cities,

our desk and calendar clear, our debts
paid until summer. The smoke of piñon
seeps back inside under almost invisible
cracks, the better to smell it. All day

we take turns holding hands and counting
the years we never believed we'd make it—
the hours of skinned knees and pleading,
diapers and teenage rage and fever

in the middle of the night, and parents
dying, and Saigon, the endless guilt
of surviving. Nights, we lie touching
for hours and listen, the silent woods

so close we can hear owls diving.
These woods are not our woods,
though we hold a key to dead pine planks
laid side by side, shiplap like a dream

that lasts, a double bed that fits us
after all these years, a blunt
front-feeding stove that gives back
temporary heat for all the logs we own.

Winter Winds Cold and Blea

John Clare

Winter winds cold and blea
Chilly blows o'er the lea:
Wander not out to me,
   Jenny so fair,
Wait in thy cottage free.
   I will be there.

Wait in thy cushioned chair
Wi' thy white bosom bare.
Kisses are sweetest there:
   Leave it for me.
Free from the chilly air
   I will meet thee.

How sweet can courting prove,
How can I kiss my love
Muffled in hat and glove
   From the chill air?
Quaking beneath the grove,
   What love is there!

Lay by thy woollen vest,
Drape no cloak o'er thy breast:
Where my hand oft hath pressed,
   Pin nothing there:
Where my head droops to rest,
   Leave its bed bare.

e. e. cummings

since feeling is first
who pays any attention
to the syntax of things
will never wholly kiss you;

wholly to be a fool
while Spring is in the world

my blood approves,
and kisses are a better fate
than wisdom
lady i swear by all flowers. Don't cry
—the best gesture of my brain is less than
your eyelids' flutter which says

we are for each other: then
laugh, leaning back in my arms
for life's not a paragraph

And death i think is no parenthesis

Vergissmeinnicht

Keith Douglas

Three weeks gone and the combatants gone
returning over the nightmare ground
we found the place again, and found
the soldier sprawling in the sun.

The frowning barrel of his gun
overshadowing. As we came on
that day, he hit my tank with one
like the entry of a demon.

Look. Here in the gunpit spoil
the dishonoured picture of his girl
who has put: *Steffi. Vergissmeinnicht*
in a copybook gothic script.

We see him almost with content,
abased, and seeming to have paid
and mocked at by his own equipment
that's hard and good when he's decayed.

But she would weep to see today
how on his skin the swart flies move;
the dust upon the paper eye
and the burst stomach like a cave.

For here the lover and killer are mingled
who had one body and one heart.
And death who had the soldier singled
has done the lover mortal hurt.

Sonnet XLIII

Edna St. Vincent Millay

What lips my lips have kissed, and where, and why,
I have forgotten, and what arms have lain
Under my head till morning; but the rain
Is full of ghosts tonight, that tap and sigh
Upon the glass and listen for reply,
And in my heart there sits a quiet pain
For unremembered lads that not again
Will turn to me at midnight with a cry.
Thus in the winter stands the lonely tree,
Nor knows what birds have vanished one by one,
Yet knows its boughs more silent than before:
I cannot say what loves have come and gone,
I only know that summer sang in me
A little while, that in me sings no more.

After the Argument

Stephen Dunn

Whoever spoke first would lose something,
　　that was the stupid
　　　　unspoken rule.

The stillness would be a clamor, a capo
　　on a nerve. He'd stare
　　　　out the window,

she'd put away dishes, anything
　　for some noise. They'd sleep
　　　　in different rooms.

The trick was to speak as if you hadn't
　　spoken, a comment
　　　　so incidental

it wouldn't be counted as speech.
　　Or to touch while passing,
　　　　an accident

of clothing, billowy sleeve against
　　rolled-up cuff. They couldn't
　　　　stand hating

each other for more than one day.
Each knew this, each knew
The other's body

Would begin to lean, the voice yearn
for the familiar confluence
of breath and syllable.

When? Who first? It was Yalta, always
on some level the future,
the next time.

This time

there was a cardinal on the bird feeder;
one of them was shameless enough
to say so, the other pleased

to agree. And their sex was a knot
untying itself, a prolonged
coming loose.

The Orange

Wendy Cope

At lunchtime I bought a huge orange—
The size of it made us all laugh.
I peeled it and shared it with Robert and Dave—
They got quarters and I had a half.

And that orange, it made me so happy,
As ordinary things often do
Just lately. The shopping. A walk in the park.
This is peace and contentment. It's new.

The rest of the day was quite easy.
I did all the jobs on my list
And enjoyed them and had some time over.
I love you. I'm glad I exist.

Susquehanna

Liz Rosenberg

Those many dark nights in our wedding house.
Hundreds of them—like fireflies—
above the quiet road till dawn,
and still I can't remember even
one of the naked trips he made downstairs
to bring me back a glass of water:
aged, sagging, fly-footed one.
Then the dog would sneak into our room
and groan and settle his bones down
on the wood floor, heavily.

I knew we were all going to die
but not then, and not right away;
because in those days
there were more days to come.
I thought I could not
run out of them.

Farm Wife

R. S. Thomas

Hers is the clean apron, good for fire
Or lamp to embroider, as we talk slowly
In the long kitchen, while the white dough
Turns to pastry in the great oven,
Sweetly and surely as hay making
In a June meadow; hers are the hands,
Humble with milking, but still now
In her wide lap as though they heard
A quiet music, hers being the voice
That coaxes time back to the shadows
In the room's corners. O, hers is all
This strong body, the safe island
Where men may come, sons and lovers,
Daring the cold seas of her eyes.

After Forty Years of Marriage, She Tries a New Recipe for Hamburger Hot Dish

Leo Dangel

"How did you like it?" she asked.

"It's all right," he said.

"This is the third time I cooked
it this way. Why can't you
ever say if you like something?"

"Well if I didn't like it, I
wouldn't eat it," he said.

"You never can say anything
I cook tastes good."

"I don't know why all the time
you think I have to say it's good.
I eat it, don't I?"

"I don't think you have to say
all the time it's good, but once
in awhile you could say
you like it."

"It's all right," he said.

Those Who Love

Sara Teasdale

Those who love the most,
Do not talk of their love,
Francesca, Guinevere,
Deirdre, Iseult, Heloise,
In the fragrant gardens of heaven
Are silent, or speak if at all
Of fragile, inconsequent things.

And a woman I used to know
Who loved one man from her youth,
Against the strength of the fates
Fighting in somber pride,
Never spoke of this thing,
But hearing his name by chance,
A light would pass over her face.

Quietly

Kenneth Rexroth

Lying here quietly beside you,
My cheek against your firm, quiet thighs,
The calm music of Boccherini
Washing over us in the quiet,
As the sun leaves the housetops and goes
Out over the Pacific, quiet—
So quiet the sun moves beyond us,
So quiet as the sun always goes,
So quiet, our bodies, worn with the
Times and the penances of love, our
Brains curled, quiet in their shells, dormant,
Our hearts slow, quiet, reliable
In their interlocked rhythms, the pulse
In your thigh caressing my cheek. Quiet.

For C.W.B.

Elizabeth Bishop

I

Let us live in a lull of the long winter winds
       Where the shy, silver-antlered reindeer go
On dainty hoofs with their white rabbit friends
       Amidst the delicate flowering snow.

All of our thoughts will be fairer than doves.
       We will live upon wedding-cake frosted with sleet.
We will build us a house from two red tablecloths,
       And wear scarlet mittens on both hands and feet.

II

Let us live in the land of the whispering trees,
       Alder and aspen and poplar and birch,
Singing our prayers in a pale, sea-green breeze,
       With star-flower rosaries and moss banks for church.

All of our dreams will be clearer than glass.
       Clad in the water or sun, as you wish,
We will watch the white feet of the young morning pass
       And dine upon honey and small shiny fish.

III

Let us live where the twilight lives after the dark,
       In the deep, drowsy blue, let us make us a home.
Let us meet in the cool evening grass, with a stork
       And a whistle of willow, played by a gnome.

Half-asleep, half-awake, we shall hear, we shall know
       The soft "Miserere" the wood-swallow tolls.
We will wander away where wild raspberries grow
       And eat them for tea from two lily-white bowls.

Shorelines

Howard Moss

Someday I'll wake and hardly think of you;
You'll be some abstract deity, a myth—
Say Daphne, if you knew her as a tree.
Don't think I won't be grateful. I will be.
We'd shuck the oysters, cool them off with lime,
Spice them with Tabasco, and then scoop them up,
Who thought we were in Paradise. We were not.
Three couples and three singles shared that house
For two weeks in September. Wellfleet stayed
Remarkable that fall. And so did we.
Confessions, confidences kept us up
Half the night; the dawn birds found us still
Dead tired, clenched on the emotional,
Which led to two divorces later on,
Recriminations, torn-up loyalties,
The dreariness of things gone wrong for good.
Yet who could forget those wet, bucolic rides,
Drunk dances on the beach, the bonfires,
The sandy lobsters not quite fit to eat?
Well, there were other falls to come as bad,
But I still see us on a screened-in porch,
Dumbly determined to discover when
The tide turned and the bay sank back in mud.
We'd watch it carefully, hour after hour,

But somehow never could decide just when
The miracle occurred. Someone would run
Into the marshes yelling, "Where's the shore?"
We hardly see each other anymore.

Prayer for a Marriage

Steve Scafidi

For Kathleen

When we are old one night and the moon
arcs over the house like an antique
China saucer and the teacup sun

follows somewhere far behind
I hope the stars deepen to a shine
so bright you could read by it

if you liked and the sadnesses
we will have known go away
for awhile—in this hour or two

before sleep—and that we kiss
standing in the kitchen not fighting
gravity so much as embodying

its sweet force, and I hope we kiss
like we do today knowing so much
good is said in this primitive tongue

from the wild first surprising ones
to the lower dizzy ten thousand
infinitely slower ones—and I hope

while we stand there in the kitchen
making tea and kissing, the whistle
of the teapot wakes the neighbors.

The Master Speed

Robert Frost

No speed of wind or water rushing by
But you have speed far greater. You can climb
Back up a stream of radiance to the sky,
And back through history up the stream of time.
And you were given this swiftness, not for haste
Nor chiefly that you may go where you will,
But in the rush of everything to waste,
That you may have the power of standing still—
Off any still or moving thing you say.
Two such as you with such a master speed
Cannot be parted nor be swept away
From one another once you are agreed
That life is only life forevermore
Together wing to wing and oar to oar.

Bonnard's Nudes

Raymond Carver

His wife. Forty years he painted her.
Again and again. The nude in the last painting
the same young nude as the first. His wife.

As he remembered her young. As she was young.
His wife in her bath. At her dressing table
in front of the mirror. Undressed.

His wife with her hands under her breasts
looking out on the garden.
The sun bestowing warmth and color.

Every living thing in bloom there.
She young and tremulous and most desirable.
When she died, he painted a while longer.

A few landscapes. Then died.
And was put down next to her.
His young wife.

6

DAY'S WORK

Happiness

Raymond Carver

So early it's still almost dark out.
I'm near the window with coffee,
and the usual early morning stuff
that passes for thought.
When I see the boy and his friend
walking up the road
to deliver the newspaper.
They wear caps and sweaters,
and one boy has a bag over his shoulder.
They are so happy
they aren't saying anything, these boys.
I think if they could, they would take
each other's arm.
It's early in the morning,
and they are doing this thing together.
They come on, slowly.
The sky is taking on light,
though the moon still hangs pale over the water.
Such beauty that for a minute
death and ambition, even love,
doesn't enter into this.
Happiness. It comes on
unexpectedly. And goes beyond, really,
any early morning talk about it.

Hoeing

John Updike

I sometimes fear the younger generation will be deprived
    of the pleasures of hoeing;
      there is no knowing
how many souls have been formed by this simple exercise.

The dry earth like a great scab breaks, revealing
    moist-dark loam—
      the pea-root's home,
a fertile wound perpetually healing.

How neatly the green weeds go under!
    The blade chops the earth new.
      Ignorant the wise boy who
has never performed this simple, stupid, and useful wonder.

Some Details of Hebridean House Construction

Thomas A. Clark

the walls are built with
unmortared boulders
the external faces having
an inward slope
the corners rounded

roofs are thatched with
straw, ferns or heather
and weighted with stones
hung from heather ropes

instead of overhanging
the roof is set back
on a broad wall-top
which in the course of time
becomes mantled with
grass and verdure
which may provide
occasional browsing
for a sheep or goat

back to the wind
face to the sun
is the general
orientation

the floor is of beaten earth
and the main room is reached
by way of the byre
there are no windows and
the frugal flame of the peat
gives the only illumination
smoke wanders and finds
egress by a hole in the roof

in the outer isles the floor is covered
with white sand from the machair

a few steps ascend
the wall near the door
to enable the roof
to be thatched or roped
or the family to sit
in the summer weather
and sew, chat or knit

by the peat store
near to the doorway
is placed a large stone
for the wanderer to sit on

Relations
Old Light/New Sun/Postmistress/Earth/04421

Philip Booth

From broken dreams,
                              we wake to every day's
brave history,

the gravity
                of every moment
we wake

to let our lives
                   inhabit: *now, here, again,*
this very day,

passionate as all
                      Yeats woke in old age
to hope for, the sun

turns up, under
                 an off-shore cloudbank
spun at 700 and

some mph to meet it,
                      rosy as the cheeks
of a Chios woman

Homer may have been
                    touched by, just
as Janet

is touching, climbing
                    familiar steps, granite
locally quarried,

to work at 04421,
                    a peninsular village
spun, just as

Janet is spun,
                    into light, light appearing
to resurrect

not simply its own
                    life but the whole
improbable
      '

system, tugging
                    the planet around to
look precisely

as Janet looks,
                    alight with the gravity
of her office,

before turning
                    the key that opens up
its full

radiance:
        the familiar arrivals,
departures,

and even predictable
              orbits in which,
with excited

constancy, by how
        to each other
we're held, we keep

from spinning out
        by how to each other
we hold.

What I Learned from My Mother

Julia Kasdorf

I learned from my mother how to love
the living, to have plenty of vases on hand
in case you have to rush to the hospital
with peonies cut from the lawn, black ants
still stuck to the buds. I learned to save jars
large enough to hold fruit salad for a whole
grieving household, to cube home-canned pears
and peaches, to slice through maroon grape skins
and flick out the sexual seeds with a knife point.
I learned to attend viewings even if I didn't know
the deceased, to press the moist hands
of the living, to look in their eyes and offer
sympathy, as though I understood loss even then.
I learned that whatever we say means nothing,
what anyone will remember is that we came.
I learned to believe I had the power to ease
awful pains materially like an angel.
Like a doctor, I learned to create
from another's suffering my own usefulness, and once
you know how to do this, you can never refuse.
To every house you enter, you must offer
healing: a chocolate cake you baked yourself,
the blessing of your voice, your chaste touch.

To be of use

Marge Piercy

The people I love the best
jump into work head first
without dallying in the shallows
and swim off with sure strokes almost out of sight.
They seem to become natives of that element,
the black sleek heads of seals
bouncing like half-submerged balls.

I love people who harness themselves, an ox to a heavy cart,
who pull like water buffalo, with massive patience,
who strain in the mud and the muck to move things forward,
who do what has to be done, again and again.

I want to be with people who submerge
in the task, who go into the fields to harvest
and work in a row and pass the bags along,
who are not parlor generals and field deserters
but move in a common rhythm
when the food must come in or the fire be put out.

The work of the world is common as mud.
Botched, it smears the hands, crumbles to dust.
But the thing worth doing well done
has a shape that satisfies, clean and evident.
Greek amphoras for wine or oil,

Hopi vases that held corn, are put in museums
but you know they were made to be used.
The pitcher cries for water to carry
and a person for work that is real.

No Tool or Rope or Pail

Bob Arnold

It hardly mattered what time of year
We passed by their farmhouse,
They never waved,
This old farm couple
Usually bent over in the vegetable garden
Or walking the muddy dooryard
Between house and red-weathered barn.
They would look up, see who was passing,
Then look back down, ignorant to the event.
We would always wave nonetheless,
Before you dropped me off at work
Further up on the hill,
Toolbox rattling in the backseat,
And then again on the way home
Later in the day, the pale sunlight
High up in their pasture,
Our arms out the window,
Cooling ourselves.
And it was that one midsummer evening
We drove past and caught them sitting
Together on the front porch
At ease, chores done,
The tangle of cats and kittens
Cleaning themselves of fresh spilled milk
On the barn door ramp;

We drove by and they looked up—
The first time I've ever seen their
Hands free of any work,
No tool or rope or pail—
And they waved.

Ox Cart Man

Donald Hall

In October of the year,
he counts potatoes dug from the brown field,
counting the seed, counting
the cellar's portion out,
and bags the rest on the cart's floor.

He packs wool sheared in April, honey
in combs, linen, leather
tanned from deerhide,
and vinegar in a barrel
hooped by hand at the forge's fire.

He walks by his ox's head, ten days
to Portsmouth Market, and sells potatoes,
and the bag that carried potatoes,
flaxseed, birch brooms, maple sugar, goose
feathers, yarn.

When the cart is empty he sells the cart.
When the cart is sold he sells the ox,
harness and yoke, and walks
home, his pockets heavy
with the year's coin for salt and taxes,

and at home by fire's light in November cold
stitches new harness
for next year's ox in the barn,
and carves the yoke, and saws planks
building the cart again.

Girl on a Tractor

Joyce Sutphen

I knew the names of all the cows before
I knew my alphabet, but no matter the
subject; I had mastery of it, and when
it came time to help in the fields, I
learned to drive a tractor at just the right
speed, so that two men, walking
on either side of the moving wagon
could each lift a bale, walk towards
the steadily arriving platform and
simultaneously hoist the hay onto
the rack, walk to the next bale, lift,
turn, and find me there, exactly where
I should be, my hand on the throttle,
carefully measuring out the pace.

Soybeans

Thomas Alan Orr

The October air was warm and musky, blowing
Over brown fields, heavy with the fragrance
Of freshly combined beans, the breath of harvest.

He was pulling a truckload onto the scales
At the elevator near the rail siding north of town
When a big Cadillac drove up. A man stepped out,
Wearing a three-piece suit and a gold pinky ring.
The man said he had just invested a hundred grand
In soybeans and wanted to see what they looked like.

The farmer stared at the man and was quiet, reaching
For the tobacco in the rear pocket of his jeans,
Where he wore *his* only ring, a threadbare circle rubbed
By working cans of dip and long hours on the backside
Of a hundred acre run. He scooped up a handful
Of small white beans, the pearls of the prairie, saying:

Soybeans look like a foot of water on the field in April
When you're ready to plant and can't get in;
Like three kids at the kitchen table
Eating macaroni and cheese five nights in a row;
Or like a broken part on the combine when
Your credit with the implement dealer is nearly tapped.

Soybeans look like prayers bouncing off the ceiling
When prices on the Chicago grain market start to drop;
Or like your old man's tears when you tell him
How much the land might bring for subdivisions.
Soybeans look like the first good night of sleep in weeks
When you unload at the elevator and the kids get Christmas.

He spat a little juice on the tire of the Cadillac,
Laughing despite himself and saying to the man:
Now maybe you can tell me what a hundred grand looks like.

Landing Pattern

Philip Appleman

We give them our lives
in the fog, the men with voices
out of Midwestern computers;
arms like kites, we touch
the sinister ice on the wings, our heads
always up there, forward, brains
in the cockpit, wired
to the banks of instruments, blinking
indicators, what has gone wrong
with our lives, the red lights
chattering, what is it slipping
out of our beautiful blood,
out of the ache in our marrow,
tugging us all the way home
to treetops, houses, dogs
in friendly gardens, the homely love
of grass: squeezing our eyes to feel
the solid-state components, rock
and soil, magnetic iron
moving through our veins,
mothering elements pulling
flesh to ashes:
the gentle thump,
and they've done it again, the voices
out of Midwestern

computers, brought us in
to the promises of runways,
one more perfect landing
in our beautiful blood.

Mae West

Edward Field

She comes on drenched in a perfume called Self-Satisfaction
from feather boa to silver pumps.

She does not need to be loved by you
though she'll give you credit for good taste.
Just because you say you love her
she's not throwing herself at your feet in gratitude.

Every other star reveals how worthless she feels
by crying when the hero says he loves her,
or how unhoped-for the approval is
when the audience applauds her big number—
but Mae West takes it as her due:
she knows she's good.

She expects the best for herself
and knows she's worth what she costs
and she costs plenty—
she's not giving anything away.

She enjoys her admirers, fat daddy or muscleman,
and doesn't confuse vanity and sex,
though she never turns down pleasure,
lapping it up.

Above all she enjoys her self,
swinging her body that says, Me, me, me, me,
Why not have a good time?
As long as you amuse me, go on,
I like you slobbering over my hand, big boy—
I have a right to.

Most convincing, we know all this
not by her preaching
but by her presence—it's no act.
Every word and look and movement
spells Independence:
she likes being herself.

And we who don't
can only look on, astonished.

Hay for the Horses

Gary Snyder

He had driven half the night
From far down San Joaquin
Through Mariposa, up the
Dangerous Mountain roads,
And pulled in at eight a.m.
With his big truckload of hay
    behind the barn.
With winch and ropes and hooks
We stacked the bales up clean
To splintery redwood rafters
High in the dark, flecks of alfalfa
Whirling through shingle-cracks of light,
Itch of haydust in the
    sweaty shirt and shoes.
At lunchtime under Black oak
Out in the hot corral,
—The old mare nosing lunchpails,
Grasshoppers crackling in the weeds—
 "I'm sixty-eight" he said,
"I first bucked hay when I was seventeen.
 I thought, that day I started,
I sure would hate to do this all my life.
And dammit, that's just what
I've gone and done."

7

SONS AND DAUGHTERS

Masterworks of Ming

Kay Ryan

Ming, Ming,
such a lovely
thing blue
and white

bowls and
basins glow
in museum
light

they would
be lovely
filled with
rice or
water

so nice
adjunct
to dinner

or washing
a daughter

a small
daughter
of course
since it's
a small basin

first you
would put
one then

the other
end in

Bess

Linda Pastan

When Bess, the landlord's black-eyed
daughter, waited for her highwayman
in the poem I learned by breathless
heart at twelve, it occurred to me

for the first time that my mild-eyed
mother Bess might have a life
all her own—a secret past
I couldn't enter, except in dreams.

That single sigh of a syllable
has passed like a keepsake
to this newest child, wrapped now
in the silence of sleep.

And in the dream I enter,
I could be holding my infant mother
in my arms: the same wide cheekbones,
the name indelible as a birthmark.

A Little Tooth

Thomas Lux

Your baby grows a tooth, then two,
and four, and five, then she wants some meat
directly from the bone. It's all

over: she'll learn some words, she'll fall
in love with cretins, dolts, a sweet
talker on his way to jail. And you,

your wife, get old, flyblown, and rue
nothing. You did, you loved, your feet
are sore. It's dusk. Your daughter's tall.

Sonnet XXXVII

William Shakespeare

As a decrepit father takes delight
To see his active child do deeds of youth,
So I, made lame by Fortune's dearest spite,
Take all my comfort of thy worth and truth;
For whether beauty, birth, or wealth, or wit,
Or any of these all, or all, or more,
Entitled in thy parts, do crowned sit,
I make my love engrafted to this store:
So then I am not lame, poor, nor despised,
Whilst that this shadow doth such substance give
That I in thy abundance am sufficed
And by a part of all thy glory live.
 Look, what is best, that best I wish in thee:
 This wish I have; then ten times happy me!

Egg

C. G. Hanzlicek

I'm scrambling an egg for my daughter.
"Why are you always whistling?" she asks.
"Because I'm happy."
And it's true,
Though it stuns me to say it aloud;
There was a time when I wouldn't
Have seen it as my future.
It's partly a matter
Of who is there to eat the egg:
The self fallen out of love with itself
Through the tedium of familiarity,
Or this little self,
So curious, so hungry,
Who emerged from the woman I love,
A woman who loves me in a way
I've come to think I deserve,
Now that it arrives from outside me.
Everything changes, we're told,
And now the changes are everywhere:
The house with its morning light
That fills me like a revelation,
The yard with its trees
That cast a bit more shade each summer,
The love of a woman
That both is and isn't confounding,

And the love
Of this clamor of questions at my waist.
Clamor of questions,
You clamor of answers,
Here's your egg.

Rolls-Royce Dreams

Ginger Andrews

Using salal leaves for money,
my youngest sister and I
paid an older sister
to taxi an abandoned car
in our backyard. Our sister
knew how to shift gears,
turn smoothly with a hand signal,
and make perfect screeching stop sounds.

We drove to the beach,
to the market, to Sunday School,
past our would-be boyfriends' houses,
to any town, anywhere.
We shopped for expensive clothes everywhere.
Our sister would open our doors
and say, *Meter's runnin' ladies,*
but take your time.

We rode all over in that ugly green Hudson
with its broken front windshield, springs poking
through its back seat, blackberry vines growing
through rusted floorboards;
with no wheels, no tires, taillights busted,
headlights missing, and gas gauge on empty.

My Life Before I Knew It

Lawrence Raab

I liked rainy days
when you didn't have to go outside and play.
At night I'd tell my sister
there were snakes under her bed.
When I mowed the lawn I imagined being famous.
Cautious and stubborn, unwilling to fail,
I knew for certain what I didn't want to know.

I hated to dance, I hated baseball,
and collected airplane cards instead.
I learned to laugh at jokes I didn't get.
The death of Christ moved me,
but only at the end of *Ben-Hur.*
I thought Henry Mancini was a great composer.

My secret desire was to own a collie
who would walk with me in the woods
when the leaves were falling
and I was thinking about writing the stories
that would make me famous.

Sullen, overweight, melancholy,
writers didn't have to be good at sports.
They stayed inside for long periods of time.
They often wore glasses. But strangers

were moved by what they accomplished
and wrote them letters. One day

one of those strangers would introduce
herself to me, and then
the life I'd never been able to foresee
would begin, and everything
before I became myself would appear
necessary to the rest of the story.

After Work

Richard Jones

Coming up from the subway
into the cool Manhattan evening,
I feel rough hands on my heart—
women in the market yelling
over rows of tomatoes and peppers,
old men sitting on a stoop playing cards,
cabbies cursing each other with fists
while the music of church bells
sails over the street,
and the father, angry and tired
after working all day,
embracing his little girl,
kissing her,
mi vida, mi corazón,
brushing the hair out of her eyes
so she can see.

I Stop Writing the Poem

Tess Gallagher

to fold the clothes. No matter who lives
or who dies, I'm still a woman.
I'll always have plenty to do.
I bring the arms of his shirt
together. Nothing can stop
our tenderness. I'll get back
to the poem. I'll get back to being
a woman. But for now
there's a shirt, a giant shirt
in my hands, and somewhere a small girl
standing next to her mother
watching to see how it's done.

Franklin Hyde,
Who caroused in the Dirt and was corrected by His Uncle.

Hilaire Belloc

His Uncle came on Franklin Hyde
Carousing in the Dirt.
He Shook him hard from Side to Side
And
Hit him till it Hurt,

Exclaiming, with a Final Thud,
'Take that! Abandoned Boy!
For Playing with Disgusting Mud
As though it were a Toy!'

Moral

From Franklin Hyde's adventure, learn
To pass your Leisure Time
In Cleanly Merriment, and turn
From Mud and Ooze and Slime
And every form of Nastiness—
But, on the other Hand,
Children in ordinary Dress
May always play with Sand.

Manners

For a Child of 1918

Elizabeth Bishop

My grandfather said to me
as we sat on the wagon seat,
"Be sure to remember to always
speak to everyone you meet."

We met a stranger on foot.
My grandfather's whip tapped his hat.
"Good day, sir. Good day. A fine day."
And I said it and bowed where I sat.

Then we overtook a boy we knew
with his big pet crow on his shoulder.
"Always offer everyone a ride;
don't forget that when you get older,"

my grandfather said. So Willy
climbed up with us, but the crow
gave a "Caw!" and flew off. I was worried.
How would he know where to go?

But he flew a little way at a time
from fence post to fence post, ahead;
and when Willy whistled he answered.
"A fine bird," my grandfather said,

"and he's well brought up. See, he answers
nicely when he's spoken to.
Man or beast, that's good manners.
Be sure that you both always do."

When automobiles went by,
the dust hid the people's faces,
but we shouted "Good day! Good day!
Fine day!" at the top of our voices.

When we came to Hustler Hill,
he said that the mare was tired,
so we all got down and walked,
as our good manners required.

September, the First Day of School

Howard Nemerov

I

My child and I hold hands on the way to school,
And when I leave him at the first-grade door
He cries a little but is brave; he does
Let go. My selfish tears remind me how
I cried before that door a life ago.
I may have had a hard time letting go.

Each fall the children must endure together
What every child also endures alone:
Learning the alphabet, the integers,
Three dozen bits and pieces of a stuff
So arbitrary, so peremptory,
That worlds invisible and visible

Bow down before it, as in Joseph's dream
The sheaves bowed down and then the stars bowed down
Before the dreaming of a little boy.
That dream got him such hatred of his brothers
As cost the greater part of life to mend,
And yet great kindness came of it in the end.

II

A school is where they grind the grain of thought,
And grind the children who must mind the thought.
It may be those two grindings are but one,
As from the alphabet come Shakespeare's plays,
As from the integers comes Euler's Law,
As from the whole, inseparably, the lives,

The shrunken lives that have not been set free
By law or by poetic phantasy.
But may they be. My child has disappeared
Behind the schoolroom door. And should I live
To see his coming forth, a life away,
I know my hope, but do not know its form

Nor hope to know it. May the fathers he finds
Among his teachers have a care of him
More than his father could. How that will look
I do not know, I do not need to know.
Even our tears belong to ritual.
But may great kindness come of it in the end.

First Lesson

Philip Booth

Lie back, daughter, let your head
be tipped back in the cup of my hand.
Gently, and I will hold you. Spread
your arms wide, lie out on the stream
and look high at the gulls. A dead-
man's-float is face down. You will dive
and swim soon enough where this tidewater
ebbs to the sea. Daughter, believe
me, when you tire on the long thrash
to your island, lie up, and survive.
As you float now, where I held you
and let go, remember when fear
cramps your heart what I told you:
lie gently and wide to the light-year
stars, lie back, and the sea will hold you.

Childhood

Barbara Ras

Driving the last stretch before the home stretch, past the lake,
geese in the road, hard to tell if they're crossing or just now
milling around like consultants in the same old way/new way
    debates,
probing the air with their long necks to see if it's still penetrable
or if maybe just ahead some future has locked into place
like the kind of walls you hit in your childhood, new rules
popping up unexpectedly in a new place—don't say "Hey"
at your aunt's, no sitting on the edge of the bed at your
    grandmother's.
You wait, feeling the distance you felt as a kid watching from the
    back seat,
your grandfather's Kaiser, where you went the way you went
    everywhere,
empty-handed. It is the fifties.
You've been told, "Children should be seen
and not heard," but not why, and because you want to please
and because you have nothing to say to your grandparents in front
who may or may not take you to the dairy bar with the huge milk
    bottle rising
out of the building, which no one in your family has remarked on
    so you too
take for granted, you sit quietly, a tidy right angle on the green
    velveteen
the color of canned pea soup without ham you like,

and stretch out a toe to reach the fattish rope slung from side to
     side
on the back of the front seat, and instead of wondering what it's for,
you hope as hard as you can you'll stop at the airport
and get to hang on the diamond chain links of the fence
and if you're lucky watch a plane take off on its scary monster
     propellers.
But now in another car waiting for geese to waddle to the left
or the right, you think about those upholstered ropes,
whether they were there to grab in case of accident or fright
or to stop from swaying too far into the body beside you,
and you wonder whatever happened to them,
whether they went the way of embroidered hankies, candy
     cigarettes,
gone with the way the moon hits your eye like a big pizza pie,
gone with afternoons a five-year-old could walk downtown to
     the library
alone and back, gone with key skates, three-speed bikes, gone
     with days
when children owned the streets.

Waving Good-Bye

Gerald Stern

I wanted to know what it was like before we
had voices and before we had bare fingers and before we
had minds to move us through our actions
and tears to help us over our feelings,
so I drove my daughter through the snow to meet her friend
and filled her car with suitcases and hugged her
as an animal would, pressing my forehead against her,
walking in circles, moaning, touching her cheek,
and turned my head after them as an animal would,
watching helplessly as they drove over the ruts,
her smiling face and her small hand just visible
over the giant pillows and coat hangers
as they made their turn into the empty highway.

Family Reunion

Maxine Kumin

The week in August you come home,
adult, professional, aloof,
we roast and carve the fatted calf
—in our case home-grown pig, the chine
garlicked and crisped, the applesauce
hand-pressed. Hand-pressed the greengage wine.

Nothing is cost-effective here.
The peas, the beets, the lettuces
hand sown, are raised to stand apart.
The electric fence ticks like the slow heart
of something we fed and bedded for a year,
then killed with kindness's one bullet
and paid Jake Mott to do the butchering.

In winter we lure the birds with suet,
thaw lungs and kidneys for the cat.
Darlings, it's all a circle from the ring
of wire that keeps the raccoons from the corn
to the gouged pine table that we lounge around,
distressed before any of you was born.

Benign and dozy from our gluttonies,
the candles down to stubs, defenses down,
love leaking out unguarded the way
juice dribbles from the fence when grounded

by grass stalks or a forgotten hoe,
how eloquent, how beautiful you seem!

Wearing our gestures, how wise you grow,
ballooning to overfill our space,
the almost-parents of your parents now.
So briefly having you back to measure us
is harder than having let you go.

8

LANGUAGE

A Primer of the Daily Round

Howard Nemerov

A peels an apple, while B kneels to God,
C telephones to D, who has a hand
On E's knee, F coughs, G turns up the sod
For H's grave, I do not understand
But J is bringing one clay pigeon down
While K brings down a nightstick on L's head,
And M takes mustard, N drives into town,
O goes to bed with P, and Q drops dead,
R lies to S, but happens to be heard
By T, who tells U not to fire V
For having to give W the word
That X is now deceiving Y with Z,
  Who happens just now to remember A
  Peeling an apple somewhere far away.

The Possessive Case

Lisel Mueller

Your father's mustache
My brother's keeper
La plume de ma tante
Le monocle de mon oncle
His Master's Voice
Son of a bitch
Charley's Aunt
Lady Chatterley's Lover
     The Prince of Wales
     The Duchess of Windsor
     The Count of Monte Cristo
     The Emperor of Ice Cream
     The Marquis de Sade
     The Queen of the Night
        Mozart's Requiem
        Beethoven's Ninth
        Bach's B-Minor Mass
        Schubert's Unfinished
        Krapp's Last Tape
        Custer's Last Stand
        Howards End
        Finnegans Wake
            The March of Time
            The Ides of March
            The Auroras of Autumn
            The winter of our discontent

The hounds of spring
The Hound of Heaven
Dante's Inferno
Vergil's Aeneid
Homer's Iliad
The Fall of the City
The Decline of the West
The Birth of a Nation
The Declaration of Independence
The ride of Paul Revere
The Pledge of Allegiance
The Spirit of '76
The Age of Reason
The Century of the Common Man
The Psychopathology of Everyday Life
Portnoy's Complaint
Whistler's Mother
The Sweetheart of Sigma Chi
The whore of Babylon
The Bride of Frankenstein
The French Lieutenant's Woman
A Room of One's Own
Bluebeard's Castle
Plato's cave
Santa's workshop
Noah's ark
The House of the Seven Gables
The Dance of the Seven Veils
Anitra's Dance
The Moor's Pavane
My Papa's Waltz
Your father's mustache

The Icelandic Language

Bill Holm

In this language, no industrial revolution;
no pasteurized milk; no oxygen, no telephone;
only sheep, fish, horses, water falling.
The middle class can hardly speak it.

In this language, no flush toilet; you stumble
through dark and rain with a handful of rags.
The door groans; the old smell comes
up from under the earth to meet you.

But this language believes in ghosts;
chairs rock by themselves under the lamp; horses
neigh inside an empty gully, nothing
at the bottom but moonlight and black rocks.

The woman with marble hands whispers
this language to you in your sleep; faces
come to the window and sing rhymes; old ladies
wind long hair, hum, tat, fold jam inside pancakes.

In this language, you can't chit-chat
holding a highball in your hand, can't
even be polite. Once the sentence starts its course,
all your grief and failure come clear at last.

Old inflections move from case to case,
gender to gender, softening consonants, darkening
vowels, till they sound like the sea moving
icebergs back and forth in its mouth.

The Fantastic Names of Jazz

Hayden Carruth

Zoot Sims, Joshua Redman,
Billie Holiday, Pete Fountain,
Fate Marable, Ivie Anderson,
Meade Lux Lewis, Mezz Mezzrow,
Manzie Johnson, Marcus Roberts,
Omer Simeon, Miff Mole, Sister
Rosetta Tharpe, Freddie Slack,
Thelonious Monk, Charlie Teagarden,
Max Roach, Paul Celestin, Muggsy
Spanier, Boomie Richman, Panama
Francis, Abdullah Ibrahim, Piano
Red, Champion Jack Dupree,
Cow Cow Davenport, Shirley Horn,
Cedar Walton, Sweets Edison,
Jaki Byard, John Heard, Joy Harjo,
Pinetop Smith, Tricky Sam
Nanton, Major Holley, Stuff Smith,
Bix Beiderbecke, Bunny Berigan,
Mr. Cleanhead Vinson, Ruby Braff,
Cootie Williams, Cab Calloway,
Lockjaw Davis, Chippie Hill,
And of course Jelly Roll Morton.

Ode to the Medieval Poets

W. H. Auden

Chaucer, Langland, Douglas, Dunbar, with all your
brother Anons, how on earth did you ever manage,
    without anaesthetics or plumbing,
      in daily peril from witches, warlocks,

lepers, The Holy Office, foreign mercenaries
burning as they came, to write so cheerfully,
    with no grimaces of self-pathos?
      Long-winded you could be but not vulgar,

bawdy but not grubby, your raucous flytings
sheer high-spirited fun, whereas our makers,
    beset by every creature comfort,
      immune, they believe, to all superstitions,

even at their best are so often morose or
kinky, petrified by their gorgon egos.
    We all ask, but I doubt if anyone
      can really say why all age-groups should find our

Age quite so repulsive. Without its heartless
engines, though, you could not tenant my book-shelves,
    on hand to delect my ear and chuckle
      my sad flesh: I would gladly just now be

turning out verses to applaud a thundery
jovial June when the judas-tree is in blossom,
    but am forbidden by the knowledge
      that you would have wrought them so much better.

Sweater Weather:
A Love Song to Language

Sharon Bryan

Never better, mad as a hatter,
right as rain, might and main,
hanky panky, hot toddy,

hoity-toity, cold shoulder,
bowled over, rolling in clover,
low blow, no soap, hope

against hope, pay the piper,
liar liar pants on fire,
high and dry, shoo-fly pie,

fiddle-faddle, fit as a fiddle,
sultan of swat, muskrat
ramble, fat and sassy,

flimflam, happy as a clam,
cat's pajamas, bee's knees,
peas in a pod, pleased as punch,

pretty as a picture, nothing much,
lift the latch, double Dutch,
helter-skelter, hurdy-gurdy,

early bird, feathered friend,
dumb cluck, buck up,
shilly-shally, willy-nilly,

roly-poly, holy moly,
loose lips sink ships,
spitting image, nip in the air,

hale and hearty, part and parcel,
upsy-daisy, lazy days,
maybe baby, up to snuff,

flibbertigibbet, honky-tonk,
spic and span, handyman,
cool as a cucumber, blue moon,

high as a kite, night and noon,
love me or leave me, seventh heaven,
up and about, over and out.

9

A GOOD LIFE

Emily Dickinson

We grow accustomed to the Dark—
When Light is put away—
As when the Neighbor holds the Lamp
To witness her Goodbye—

A Moment—We uncertain step
For newness of the night—
Then—fit our Vision to the Dark—
And meet the Road—erect—

And so of larger—Darknesses—
Those Evenings of the Brain—
When not a Moon disclose a sign—
Or Star—come out—within—

The Bravest—grope a little—
And sometimes hit a Tree
Directly in the Forehead—
But as they learn to see—

Either the Darkness alters—
Or something in the sight
Adjusts itself to Midnight—
And Life steps almost straight.

A Ritual to Read to Each Other

William Stafford

If you don't know the kind of person I am
and I don't know the kind of person you are
a pattern that others made may prevail in the world
and following the wrong god home we may miss our star.

For there is many a small betrayal in the mind,
a shrug that lets the fragile sequence break
sending with shouts the horrible errors of childhood
storming out to play through the broken dyke.

And as elephants parade holding each elephant's tail,
but if one wanders the circus won't find the park,
I call it cruel and maybe the root of all cruelty
to know what occurs but not recognize the fact.

And so I appeal to a voice, to something shadowy,
a remote important region in all who talk:
though we could fool each other, we should consider—
lest the parade of our mutual life get lost in the dark.

For it is important that awake people be awake,
or a breaking line may discourage them back to sleep;
the signals we give—yes or no, or maybe—
should be clear: the darkness around us is deep.

Courage

Anne Sexton

It is in the small things we see it.
The child's first step,
as awesome as an earthquake.
The first time you rode a bike,
wallowing up the sidewalk.
The first spanking when your heart
went on a journey all alone.
When they called you crybaby
or poor or fatty or crazy
and made you into an alien,
you drank their acid
and concealed it.

Later,
if you faced the death of bombs and bullets
you did not do it with a banner,
you did it with only a hat to
cover your heart.
You did not fondle the weakness inside you
though it was there.
Your courage was a small coal
that you kept swallowing.
If your buddy saved you
and died himself in so doing,
then his courage was not courage,
it was love; love as simple as shaving soap.

Later,
if you have endured a great despair,
then you did it alone,
getting a transfusion from the fire,
picking the scabs off your heart,
then wringing it out like a sock.
Next, my kinsman, you powdered your sorrow,
you gave it a back rub
and then you covered it with a blanket
and after it had slept a while
it woke to the wings of the roses
and was transformed.

Later,
when you face old age and its natural conclusion
your courage will still be shown in the little ways,
each spring will be a sword you'll sharpen,
those you love will live in a fever of love,
and you'll bargain with the calendar
and at the last moment
when death opens the back door
you'll put on your carpet slippers
and stride out.

Sometimes

Sheenagh Pugh

Sometimes things don't go, after all,
from bad to worse. Some years, muscadel
faces down frost; green thrives; the crops don't fail,
sometimes a man aims high, and all goes well.

A people sometimes will step back from war;
elect an honest man; decide they care
enough, that they can't leave some stranger poor.
Some men become what they were born for.

Sometimes our best efforts do not go
amiss; sometimes we do as we meant to.
The sun will sometimes melt a field of sorrow
that seemed hard frozen: may it happen for you.

Leisure

W. H. Davies

What is this life if, full of care,
We have no time to stand and stare?

No time to stand beneath the boughs
And stare as long as sheep or cows.

No time to see, when woods we pass,
Where squirrels hide their nuts in grass.

No time to see, in broad daylight,
Streams full of stars, like skies at night.

No time to turn at Beauty's glance,
And watch her feet, how they can dance.

No time to wait till her mouth can
Enrich that smile her eyes began.

A poor life this if, full of care,
We have no time to stand and stare.

the way it is now

Charles Bukowski

I'll tell you
I've lived with some gorgeous women
and I was so bewitched by those
beautiful creatures that
my eyebrows twitched.

but I'd rather drive to New York
backwards
than to live with any of them
again.

the next classic stupidity
will be the history
of those fellows
who inherit my female
legacies.

in their case
as in mine
they will find
that madness
is caused by not
being often enough
alone.

A Secret Life

Stephen Dunn

Why you need to have one
is not much more mysterious than
why you don't say what you think
at the birth of an ugly baby.
Or, you've just made love
and feel you'd rather have been
in a dark booth where your partner
was nodding, whispering yes, yes,
you're brilliant. The secret life
begins early, is kept alive
by all that's unpopular
in you, all that you know
a Baptist, say, or some other
accountant would object to.
It becomes what you'd most protect
if the government said you can protect
one thing, all else is ours.
When you write late at night
it's like a small fire
in a clearing, it's what
radiates and what can hurt
if you get too close to it.
It's why your silence is a kind of truth.
Even when you speak to your best friend,
the one who'll never betray you,
you always leave out one thing;
a secret life is that important.

Lost

David Wagoner

Stand still. The trees ahead and bushes beside you
Are not lost. Wherever you are is called Here,
And you must treat it as a powerful stranger,
Must ask permission to know it and be known.
The forest breathes. Listen. It answers,
I have made this place around you.
If you leave it, you may come back again, saying Here.
No two trees are the same to Raven.
No two branches are the same to Wren.
If what a tree or a bush does is lost on you,
You are surely lost. Stand still. The forest knows
Where you are. You must let it find you.

Sonnet XXV

William Shakespeare

Let those who are in favour with their stars
Of public honour and proud titles boast,
Whilst I, whom fortune of such triumph bars,
Unlook'd for joy in that I honour most.
Great princes' favourites their fair leaves spread
But as the marigold at the sun's eye,
And in themselves their pride lies buried,
For at a frown they in their glory die.
The painful warrior famoused for fight,
After a thousand victories once foil'd,
Is from the book of honour razed quite,
And all the rest forgot for which he toil'd:
    Then happy I, that love and am beloved
    Where I may not remove nor be removed.

The Eel in the Cave

Robert Bly

Our veins are open to shadow, and our fingertips
Porous to murder. It's only the inattention
Of the prosecutors that lets us go to lunch.

Reading my old letters I notice a secret will.
It's as if another person had planned my life.
Even in the dark, someone is hitching the horses.

That doesn't mean I have done things well.
I have found so many ways to disgrace
Myself, and throw a dark cloth over my head.

Why is it our fault if we fall into desire?
The eel poking his head from his undersea cave
Entices the tiny soul falling out of Heaven.

So many invisible angels work to keep
Us from drowning; so many hands reach
Down to pull the swimmer from the water.

Even though the District Attorney keeps me
Well in mind, grace allows me sometimes
To slip into the Alhambra by night.

Wild Geese

Mary Oliver

You do not have to be good.
You do not have to walk on your knees
for a hundred miles through the desert, repenting.
You only have to let the soft animal of your body
    love what it loves.
Tell me about despair, yours, and I will tell you mine.
Meanwhile the world goes on.
Meanwhile the sun and the clear pebbles of the rain
are moving across the landscapes,
over the prairies and the deep trees,
the mountains and the rivers.
Meanwhile the wild geese, high in the clean blue air,
are heading home again.
Whoever you are, no matter how lonely,
the world offers itself to your imagination,
calls to you like the wild geese, harsh and exciting—
over and over announcing your place
in the family of things.

From the Manifesto of the Selfish

Stephen Dunn

Because altruists are the least sexy
    people on earth, unable
to say "I want" without embarrassment,

we need to take from them everything
    they give,
then ask for more,

this is how to excite them, and because
    it's exciting
to see them the least bit excited

once again we'll be doing something
    for ourselves,
who have no problem taking pleasure,

always desirous and so pleased to be
    pleased, we who above all
can be trusted to keep the balance.

Hope

Lisel Mueller

It hovers in dark corners
before the lights are turned on,
   it shakes sleep from its eyes
   and drops from mushroom gills,
      it explodes in the starry heads
      of dandelions turned sages,
         it sticks to the wings of green angels
         that sail from the tops of maples.

It sprouts in each occluded eye
of the many-eyed potato,
   it lives in each earthworm segment
   surviving cruelty,
      it is the motion that runs
      from the eyes to the tail of a dog,
         it is the mouth that inflates the lungs
         of the child that has just been born.

It is the singular gift
we cannot destroy in ourselves,
the argument that refutes death,
the genius that invents the future,
all we know of God.

It is the serum which makes us swear
not to betray one another;
it is in this poem, trying to speak.

The Three Goals

David Budbill

The first goal is to see the thing itself
in and for itself, to see it simply and clearly
for what it is.
                No symbolism, please.

The second goal is to see each individual thing
as unified, as one, with all the other
ten thousand things.
                In this regard, a little wine helps a lot.

The third goal is to grasp the first and the second goals,
to see the universal and the particular,
simultaneously.
                Regarding this one, call me when you get it.

Vermeer

Howard Nemerov

Taking what is, and seeing it as it is,
Pretending to no heroic stances or gestures,
Keeping it simple; being in love with light
And the marvelous things that light is able to do,
How beautiful! a modesty which is
Seductive extremely, the care for daily things.

At one for once with sunlight falling through
A leaded window, the holy mathematic
Plays out the cat's cradle of relation
Endlessly; even the inexorable
Domesticates itself and becomes charm.

If I could say to you, and make it stick,
A girl in a red hat, a woman in blue
Reading a letter, a lady weighing gold . . .
If I could say this to you so you saw,
And knew, and agreed that this was how it was
In a lost city across the sea of years,
I think we should be for one moment happy
In the great reckoning of those little rooms
Where the weight of life has been lifted and made light,
Or standing invisible on the shore opposed,
Watching the water in the foreground dream
Reflectively, taking a view of Delft
As it was, under a wide and darkening sky.

Repression

C. K. Williams

More and more lately, as, not even minding the slippages yet, the
    aches and sad softenings,
I settle into my other years, I notice how many of what I once
    thought were evidences of repression,
sexual or otherwise, now seem, in other people anyway, to be
    varieties of dignity, withholding, tact,
and sometimes even in myself, certain patiences I would have
    once called lassitude, indifference,
now seem possibly to be if not the rewards then at least the
    unsuspected, undreamed-of conclusions
to many of the even-then-preposterous self-evolved disciplines,
    rigors, almost mortifications
I inflicted on myself in my starting-out days, improvement days,
    days when the idea alone of psychic peace,
of intellectual, of emotional quiet, the merest hint, would have
    meant inconceivable capitulation.

Weather

Linda Pastan

Because of the menace
your father opened
like a black umbrella
and held high
over your childhood
blocking the light,
your life now seems

to you exceptional
in its simplicities.
You speak of this,
throwing the window open
on a plain spring day,
dazzling
after such a winter.

Moderation Is Not a Negation of Intensity, But Helps Avoid Monotony

John Tagliabue

Will you stop for a while, stop trying to pull yourself
        together
for some clear "meaning"—some momentary summary?
        no one
can have poetry or dances, prayers or climaxes all day;
        the ordinary
blankness of little dramatic consciousness is good for the
        health sometimes,
only Dostoevsky can be Dostoevskian at such long
        long tumultuous stretches;
look what that intensity did to poor great Van Gogh!;
        linger, lunge,
scrounge and be stupid, that doesn't take much centering
        of one's forces;
as wise Whitman said "lounge and invite the soul." Get
        enough sleep;
and not only because (as Cocteau said) "poetry is the
        literature of sleep";
be a dumb bell for a few minutes at least; we don't want
        Sunday church bells
        ringing constantly.

Emily Dickinson

Tell all the Truth but tell it slant—
Success in Circuit lies
Too bright for our infirm Delight
The Truth's superb surprise
As Lightning to the Children eased
With explanation kind
The Truth must dazzle gradually
Or every man be blind—

Emily Dickinson

The Props assist the House
Until the House is built
And then the Props withdraw
And adequate, erect,
The House support itself
And cease to recollect
The Auger and the Carpenter—
Just such a retrospect
Hath the perfected Life—
A past of Plank and Nail
And slowness—then the Scaffolds drop
Affirming it a Soul.

10

BEASTS

Little Citizen, Little Survivor

Hayden Carruth

A brown rat has taken up residence with me.
A little brown rat with pinkish ears and lovely
almond-shaped eyes. He and his wife live
in the woodpile by my back door, and they are
so equal I cannot tell which is which when they
poke their noses out of the crevices among
the sticks of firewood and then venture farther
in search of sunflower seeds spilled from the feeder.
I can't tell you, my friend, how glad I am to see them.
I haven't seen a fox for years, or a mink, or
a fisher cat, or an eagle, or a porcupine, I haven't
seen any of my old company of the woods
and the fields, we who used to live in such
close affection and admiration. Well, I remember
when the coons would tap on my window, when
the ravens would speak to me from the edge of their
little precipice. Where are they now? Everyone knows.
Gone. Scattered in this terrible dispersal. But at least
the brown rat that most people so revile and fear
and castigate has brought his wife to live with me
again. Welcome, little citizen, little survivor.
Lend me your presence, and I will lend you mine.

Her First Calf

Wendell Berry

Her fate seizes her and brings her
down. She is heavy with it. It
wrings her. The great weight
is heaved out of her. It eases.
She moves into what she has become,
sure in her fate now
as a fish free in the current.
She turns to the calf who has broken
out of the womb's water and its veil.
He breathes. She licks his wet hair.
He gathers his legs under him
and rises. He stands, and his legs
wobble. After the months
of his pursuit of her, now
they meet face to face.
From the beginnings of the world
his arrival and her welcome
have been prepared. They have always
known each other.

Bats

Randall Jarrell

A bat is born
Naked and blind and pale.
His mother makes a pocket of her tail
and catches him. He clings to her long fur
By his thumbs and toes and teeth.
And then the mother dances through the night
Doubling and looping, soaring, somersaulting—
Her baby hangs on underneath.
All night, in happiness, she hunts and flies.
Her high sharp cries
Like shining needlepoints of sound
Go out into the night, and echoing back,
Tell her what they have touched.
She hears how far it is, how big it is,
Which way it's going:
She lives by hearing.
The mother eats the moths and gnats she catches
In full flight; in full flight
The mother drinks the water of the pond
She skims across. Her baby hangs on tight.
Her baby drinks the milk she makes him
In moonlight or starlight, in mid-air.
Their single shadow, printed on the moon
Or fluttering across the stars,
Whirls on all night; at daybreak
The tired mother flaps home to her rafter.

The others all are there.
They hang themselves up by their toes,
They wrap themselves in their brown wings.
Bunched upside-down, they sleep in air.
Their sharp ears, their sharp teeth, their quick sharp faces
Are dull and slow and mild.
All the bright day, as the mother sleeps,
She folds her wings about her sleeping child.

Riding Lesson

Henry Taylor

I learned two things
from an early riding teacher.
He held a nervous filly
in one hand and gestured
with the other, saying "Listen.
Keep one leg on one side,
the other leg on the other side,
and your mind in the middle."

He turned and mounted.
She took two steps, then left
the ground, I thought for good.
But she came down hard, humped
her back, swallowed her neck,
and threw her rider as you'd
throw a rock. He rose, brushed
his pants and caught his breath,
and said, "See that's the way
to do it. When you see
they're gonna throw you, get off."

Walking the Dog

Howard Nemerov

Two universes mosey down the street
Connected by love and a leash and nothing else.
Mostly I look at lamplight through the leaves
While he mooches along with tail up and snout down,
Getting a secret knowledge through the nose
Almost entirely hidden from my sight.

We stand while he's enraptured by a bush
Till I can't stand our standing any more
And haul him off; for our relationship
Is patience balancing to this side tug
And that side drag; a pair of symbionts
Contented not to think each other's thoughts.

What else we have in common's what he taught,
Our interest in shit. We know its every state
From steaming fresh through stink to nature's way
Of sluicing it downstreet dissolved in rain
Or drying it to dust that blows away.
We move along the street inspecting it.

His sense of it is keener far than mine,
And only when he finds the place precise
He signifies by sniffing urgently
And circles thrice about, and squats, and shits,
Whereon we both with dignity walk home
And just to show who's master I write the poem.

The Excrement Poem

Maxine Kumin

It is done by us all, as God disposes, from
the least cast of worm to what must have been
in the case of the brontosaur, say, spoor
of considerable heft, something awesome.

We eat, we evacuate, survivors that we are.
I think these things each morning with shovel
and rake, drawing the risen brown buns
toward me, fresh from the horse oven, as it were,

or culling the alfalfa-green ones, expelled
in a state of ooze, through the sawdust bed
to take a serviceable form, as putty does,
so as to lift out entire from the stall.

And wheeling to it, storming up the slope,
I think of the angle of repose the manure
pile assumes, how sparrows come to pick
the redelivered grain, how inky-cap

coprinus mushrooms spring up in a downpour.
I think of what drops from us and must then
be moved to make way for the next and next.
However much we stain the world, spatter

it with our leavings, make stenches, defile
the great formal oceans with what leaks down,
trundling off today's last barrowful,
I honor shit for saying: We go on.

Stanza IV

from *Coming of Age*

Ursula Leguin

This old notebook I write in was my father's,
he never wrote in it. A grey man,
all my lifetime, with a short grey beard,
a slight man, not tall.
The other day I saw five elephants,
big elephants, with palm-trunk legs
and continents of sides, and one,
the biggest one, had bent tusks bound
about with brass. They were waiting,
patient, to be let outside
into the sunlight and the autumn air,
moving about their stall so quietly,
using the grace of great size and the gentleness,
swaying a little, silent, strong as ships.
That was a great pleasure, to see that.
And he would have liked to see the big one
    making water,
too, like a steaming river,
enough to float ten bigots in.
O there is nothing like sheer Quantity,
mountains, elephants, minds.

Destruction

Joanne Kyger

First of all do you remember the way a bear goes through
a cabin when nobody is home? He goes through
the front door. I mean he really goes *through* it. Then
he takes the cupboard off the wall and eats a can of lard.

He eats all the apples, limes, dates, bottled decaffeinated
coffee, and 35 pounds of granola. The asparagus soup cans
fall to the floor. Yum! He chomps up Norwegian crackers
stashed for the winter. And the bouillon, salt, pepper,
paprika, garlic, onions, potatoes.
                         He rips the Green Tara
poster from the wall. Tries the Coleman Mustard. Spills
the ink, tracks in the flour. Goes up stairs and takes
a shit. Rips open the water bed, eats the incense and
drinks the perfume. Knocks over the Japanese tansu
and the Persian miniature of a man on horseback watching
a woman bathing.
                 Knocks *Shelter, Whole Earth Catalogue,*
Planet Drum, Northern Mists, Truck Tracks, and
Women's Sports into the oozing water bed mess.
                                 He goes
down stairs and out the back wall. He keeps on going
for a long way and finds a good cave to sleep it all off.
Luckily he ate the whole medicine cabinet, including stash
of LSD, peyote, Psilocybin, Amanita, Benzedrine, Valium
and aspirin.

How to See Deer

Philip Booth

Forget roadside crossings.
Go nowhere with guns.
Go elsewhere your own way,

lonely and wanting. Or
stay and be early:
next to deep woods

inhabit old orchards.
All clearings promise.
Sunrise is good,

and fog before sun.
Expect nothing always;
find your luck slowly.

Wait out the windfall.
Take your good time
to learn to read ferns;

make like a turtle:
downhill toward slow water.
Instructed by heron,

drink the pure silence.
Be compassed by wind.
If you quiver like aspen

trust your quick nature:
let your ear teach you
which way to listen.

You've come to assume
protective color; now
colors reform to

new shapes in your eye.
You've learned by now
to wait without waiting;

as if it were dusk
look into light falling:
in deep relief

things even out. Be
careless of nothing. See
what you see.

Dog's Death

John Updike

She must have been kicked unseen or brushed by a car.
Too young to know much, she was beginning to learn
To use the newspapers spread on the kitchen floor
And to win, wetting there, the words, "Good dog! Good dog!"

We thought her shy malaise was a shot reaction.
The autopsy disclosed a rupture in her liver.
As we teased her with play, blood was filling her skin
And her heart was learning to lie down forever.

Monday morning, as the children were noisily fed
And sent to school, she crawled beneath the youngest's bed.
We found her twisted limp but still alive.
In the car to the vet's, on my lap, she tried

To bite my hand and died. I stroked her warm fur
And my wife called in a voice imperious with tears.
Though surrounded by love that would have upheld her,
Nevertheless she sank and, stiffening, disappeared.

Back home, we found that in the night her frame,
Drawing near to dissolution, had endured the shame
Of diarrhoea and had dragged across the floor
To a newspaper carelessly left there. *Good dog.*

Names of Horses

Donald Hall

All winter your brute shoulders strained against collars, padding
and steerhide over the ash hames, to haul
sledges of cordwood for drying through spring and summer,
for the Glenwood stove next winter, and for the simmering range.

In April you pulled cartloads of manure to spread on the fields,
dark manure of Holsteins, and knobs of your own clustered with
    oats.
All summer you mowed the grass in meadow and hayfield, the
    mowing machine
clacketing beside you, while the sun walked high in the morning;

and after noon's heat, you pulled a clawed rake through the same
    acres,
gathering stacks, and dragged the wagon from stack to stack,
and the built hayrack back, up hill to the chaffy barn,
three loads of hay a day, hanging wide from the hayrack.

Sundays you trotted the two miles to church with the light load
of a leather quartertop buggy, and grazed in the sound of hymns.
Generation on generation, your neck rubbed the window sill
of the stall, smoothing the wood as the sea smooths glass.

When you were old and lame, when your shoulders hurt bending
    to graze,
one October the man who fed you and kept you, and harnessed
    you every morning,
led you through corn stubble to sandy ground above Eagle Pond,
and dug a hole beside you where you stood shuddering in your
    skin,

and lay the shotgun's muzzle in the boneless hollow behind your
    ear,
and fired the slug into your brain, and felled you into your grave,
shoveling sand to cover you, setting goldenrod upright above you,
where by next summer a dent in the ground made your monument.

For a hundred and fifty years, in the pasture of dead horses,
roots of pine trees pushed through the pale curves of your ribs,
yellow blossoms flourished above you in autumn, and in winter
frost heaved your bones in the ground—old toilers, soil makers:

O Roger, Mackerel, Riley, Ned, Nellie, Chester, Lady Ghost.

Bison Crossing Near Mt. Rushmore

May Swenson

There is our herd of cars stopped,
staring respectfully at the line of bison crossing.
One big-fronted bull nudges his cow into a run.
She and her calf are first to cross.
In swift dignity the dark-coated caravan sweeps through
the gap our cars leave in the two-way stall
on the road to the Presidents.
The polygamous bulls guarding their families from the rear,
the honey-brown calves trotting head-to-hip
by their mothers—who are lean and muscled as bulls,
with chin tassels and curved horns—
all leap the road like a river, and run.
The strong and somber remnant of western freedom
disappears into the rough grass of the draw,
around the point of the mountain.
The bison, orderly, disciplined by the prophet-faced,
heavy-headed fathers, threading the pass
of our awestruck stationwagons, Airstreams and trailers,
if in dread of us give no sign,
go where their leaders twine them, over the prairie.
And we keep to our line,
staring, stirring, revving idling motors, moving
each behind the other, herdlike, where the highway leads.

11

FAILURE

Emily Dickinson

Success is counted sweetest
By those who ne'er succeed.
To comprehend a nectar
Requires sorest need.

Not one of all the purple Host
Who took the Flag today
Can tell the definition
So clear of Victory

As he defeated—dying—
On whose forbidden ear
The distant strains of triumph
Burst agonized and clear!

Solitude

Ella Wheeler Wilcox

Laugh, and the world laughs with you;
    Weep, and you weep alone;
For the sad old earth must borrow its mirth,
    But has trouble enough of its own.
Sing, and the hills will answer;
    Sigh, it is lost on the air;
The echoes bound to a joyful sound,
    But shrink from voicing care.

Rejoice, and men will seek you;
    Grieve, and they turn and go;
They want full measure of all your pleasure,
    But they do not need your woe.
Be glad, and your friends are many;
    Be sad, and you lose them all,—
There are none to decline your nectared wine,
    But alone you must drink life's gall.

Feast, and your halls are crowded;
    Fast, and the world goes by.
Succeed and give, and it helps you live,
    But no man can help you die.
For there is room in the halls of pleasure
    For a large and lordly train,
But one by one we must all file on
    Through the narrow aisles of pain.

Wendell Berry

The first time I remember waking up
in the night was in the winter time
when I was about six. Papa had sent
the tobacco crop to Louisville
to be sold, and we sat by the fire
that night, talking and wondering
what it would bring. It was a bad time.
A year of a man's work might be worth
nothing. And papa got up at two o'clock.
And I woke up and heard him leaving.
He saddled his horse and rode over
to the railroad, four miles, and took
the train to Louisville, and came back
in the dark that night, without a dime.

Our Lady of the Snows

Robert Hass

In white,
the unpainted statue of the young girl
on the side altar
made the quality of mercy seem scrupulous and calm.

When my mother was in a hospital drying out,
or drinking at a pace that would put her there soon,
I would slip in the side door,
light an aromatic candle,
and bargain for us both.
Or else I'd stare into the day-moon of that face
and, if I concentrated, fly.

Come down! come down!
she'd call, because I was so high.

Though mostly when I think of myself
at that age, I am standing at my older brother's closet
studying the shirts,
convinced that I could be absolutely transformed
by something I could borrow.
And the days churned by,
navigable sorrow.

The British Museum Reading Room

Louis MacNeice

Under the hive-like dome the stooping haunted readers
Go up and down the alleys, tap the cells of knowledge—
    Honey and wax, the accumulation of years—

Some on commission, some for the love of learning,
Some because they have nothing better to do
Or because they hope these walls of books will deaden
    The drumming of the demon in their ears.

Cranks, hacks, poverty-stricken scholars,
In pince-nez, period hats or romantic beards
    And cherishing their hobby or their doom
Some are too much alive and some are asleep
Hanging like bats in a world of inverted values,
Folded up in themselves in a world which is safe and silent:
    This is the British Museum Reading Room.

Out on the steps in the sun the pigeons are courting,
Puffing their ruffs and sweeping their tails or taking
    A sun-bath at their ease
And under the totem poles—the ancient terror—
Between the enormous fluted Ionic columns
There seeps from heavily jowled or hawk-like foreign faces
    The guttural sorrow of the refugees.

The Bare Arms of Trees

John Tagliabue

Sometimes when I see the bare arms of trees in the evening
I think of men who have died without love,
Of desolation and space between branch and branch,
I think of immovable whiteness and lean coldness and fear
And the terrible longing between people stretched apart as these
    branches
And the cold space between.
I think of the vastness and courage between this step and that step
Of the yearning and fear of the meeting, of the terrible desire
    held apart.
I think of the ocean of longing that moves between land and land
And between people, the space and ocean.
The bare arms of the trees are immovable, without the play of
    leaves, without the sound of wind;
I think of the unseen love and the unknown thoughts that exist
    between tree and tree
As I pass these things in the evening, as I walk.

The Sailor

Geof Hewitt

In my movie the boat goes under
And he alone survives the night in the cold ocean,
Swimming he hopes in a shoreward direction.
Daylight and he's still afloat, pawing the water
And doesn't yet know he's only fifty feet from shore.
He goes under for what will be the last time
But only a few feet down scrapes bottom.
He's suddenly a changed man and half hops, half swims
The remaining distance, hauls himself waterlogged
Partway up the beach before collapsing into sleep.
As he dreams the tide comes in
And rolls him back to sea.

A Place for Everything

Louis Jenkins

It's so easy to lose track of things. A screwdriver, for instance. "Where did I put that? I had it in my hand just a minute ago." You wander vaguely from room to room, having forgotten, by now, what you were looking for, staring into the refrigerator, the bathroom mirror . . . "I really could use a shave. . . ."

Some objects seem to disappear immediately while others never want to leave. Here is a small black plastic gizmo with a serious demeanor that turns up regularly, like a politician at public functions. It seems to be an "integral part," a kind of switch with screw holes so that it can be attached to something larger. Nobody knows what. This thing's use has been forgotten but it looks so important that no one is willing to throw it in the trash. It survives by bluff, like certain insects that escape being eaten because of their formidable appearance.

My father owned a large, three-bladed, brass propeller that he saved for years. Its worth was obvious, it was just that it lacked an immediate application since we didn't own a boat and lived hundreds of miles from any large bodies of water. The propeller survived all purges and cleanings, living, like royalty, a life of lonely privilege, mounted high on the garage wall.

The Feast

Robert Hass

The lovers loitered on the deck talking,
the men who were with men and the men who were with new
    women,
a little shrill and electric, and the wifely women
who had repose and beautifully lined faces
and coppery skin. She had taken the turkey from the oven
and her friends were talking on the deck
in the steady sunshine. She imagined them
drifting toward the food, in small groups, finishing
sentences, lifting a pickle or a sliver of turkey,
nibbling a little with unconscious pleasure. And
she imagined setting it out artfully, the white meat,
the breads, antipasto, the mushrooms and salad
arranged down the oak counter cleanly, and how they all came
as in a dance when she called them. She carved meat
and then she was crying. Then she was in darkness
crying. She didn't know what she wanted.

Nobody Knows You
When You're Down and Out

Jimmie Cox

Once I lived the life of a millionaire
Spending my money and I didn't care
Taking my friends out for a mighty fine time
Drinking high-priced liquor, champagne and wine
When I began to fall so low
I didn't have a friend and no place to go
If I ever get my hands on a dollar again
I'm gonna hold on to it till the eagle grins

Nobody knows you
When you're down and out
In your pocket, not one penny
And your friends, you haven't any
But as soon as you get on your feet again
Ev'rybody wants to be your long lost friend
It's mighty strange, without a doubt
Nobody knows you when you're down and out

the last song

Charles Bukowski

driving the freeway while
listening to the Country and Western boys
sing about a broken heart
and the honkytonk blues,
it seems that things just don't work
most of the time
and when they do it will be for a
short time
only.
well, that's not news.
nothing's news.
it's the same old thing in
disguise.
only one thing comes without a
disguise and you only see it
once, or
maybe never.
like getting hit by a freight
train.
makes us realize that all our
moaning about long lost girls
in gingham dresses
is not so important
after
all.

12

COMPLAINT

The Forsaken Wife

Elizabeth Thomas

Methinks, 'tis strange you can't afford
One *pitying Look*, one *parting Word*;
HUMANITY claims this as due,
But what's HUMANITY to you?

   Cruel Man! I am not *Blind*,
Your *Infidelity* I find;
Your want of *Love*, my *Ruin* shows,
My broken *Heart*, your broken *Vows*.
Yet maugre* all your rigid *Hate*,   *in spite of
I will be TRUE in spite of *Fate*;
And one *Preheminence* I'll claim,
To be for ever *still the same*.

   Show me a *Man* that dare be TRUE,
That dares to *suffer* what I do;
That can for *ever Sigh* unheard,
And ever *Love* without Regard:
I then will own your *Prior* Claim
To LOVE, to HONOUR, and to FAME:
But 'till that time, my Dear, adieu,
I yet SUPERIOR am to you.

Confession

Stephen Dobyns

The Nazi within me thinks it's time to take charge.
The world's a mess; people are crazy.
The Nazi within me wants windows shut tight,
new locks put on the doors. There's too much
fresh air, too much coming and going.
The Nazi within me wants more respect. He wants
the only TV camera, the only bank account,
the only really pretty girl. The Nazi within me
wants to be boss of traffic and traffic lights.
People drive too fast; they take up too much space.
The Nazi within me thinks people are getting away
with murder. He wants to be boss of murder.
He wants to be boss of bananas, boss of white bread.
The Nazi within me wants uniforms for everyone.
He wants them to wash their hands, sit up straight,
pay strict attention. He wants to make certain
they say yes when he says yes, no when he says no.
He imagines everybody sitting in straight chairs,
people all over the world sitting in straight chairs.
Are you ready? he asks them. They say they are ready.
Are you ready to be happy? he asks them. They say
they are ready to be happy. The Nazi within me wants
everyone to be happy but not too happy and definitely
not noisy. No singing, no dancing, no carrying on.

Living in the Body

Joyce Sutphen

Body is something you need in order to stay
on this planet and you only get one.
And no matter which one you get, it will not
be satisfactory. It will not be beautiful
enough, it will not be fast enough, it will
not keep on for days at a time, but will
pull you down into a sleepy swamp and
demand apples and coffee and chocolate cake.

Body is a thing you have to carry
from one day into the next. Always the
same eyebrows over the same eyes in the same
skin when you look in the mirror, and the
same creaky knee when you get up from the
floor and the same wrist under the watchband.
The changes you can make are small and
costly—better to leave it as it is.

Body is a thing that you have to leave
eventually. You know that because you have
seen others do it, others who were once like you,
living inside their pile of bones and
flesh, smiling at you, loving you,
leaning in the doorway, talking to you
for hours and then one day they
are gone. No forwarding address.

Tired As I Can Be

Bessie Jackson (Lucille Bogan)

I worked all the winter
  and I worked all fall
I've got to wait till spring
  to get my ashes hauled
    and now I'm tired
      tired as I can be
    and I'm going back home
      where these blues don't worry me

I'm a free-hearted woman
  I let you spend my dough
and you never did win
  you kept on asking for more
    and now I'm tired
      I ain't gonna do it no more
    and when I leave you this time
      you won't know where I go

My house rent's due
  they done put me out doors
and here you riding 'round here
  in a V-8 Ford
    I done got tired
      of your low-down dirty ways
    and your sister say you been dirty
      dirty all a your days

I never will forget
  when the times was good
I caught you standing out yonder
  in the piney wood
      and now I'm tired
          tired as I can be
      and I'm going back south
          to my used to be

The Iceberg Theory

Gerald Locklin

all the food critics hate iceberg lettuce.
you'd think romaine was descended from
orpheus's laurel wreath,
you'd think raw spinach had all the nutritional
benefits attributed to it by popeye,
not to mention aesthetic subtleties worthy of
verlaine and debussy.
they'll even salivate over chopped red cabbage
just to disparage poor old mr. iceberg lettuce.

I guess the problem is
it's just too common for them.
it doesn't matter that it tastes good,
has a satisfying crunchy texture,
holds its freshness,
and has crevices for the dressing,
whereas the darker, leafier varieties
are often bitter, gritty, and flat.
it just isn't different *enough,* and
it's too goddamn *american.*

of course a critic has to criticize:
a critic has to have something to say.
perhaps that's why literary critics
purport to find interesting

so much contemporary poetry
that just bores the shit out of me.

at any rate, I really enjoy a salad
with plenty of chunky iceberg lettuce,
the more the merrier,
drenched in an italian or roquefort dressing.
and the poems I enjoy are those I don't have
to pretend that I'm enjoying.

Manifesto: The Mad Farmer Liberation Front

Wendell Berry

Love the quick profit, the annual raise,
vacation with pay. Want more
of everything ready-made. Be afraid
to know your neighbors and to die.
And you will have a window in your head.
Not even your future will be a mystery
any more. Your mind will be punched in a card
and shut away in a little drawer.
When they want you to buy something
they will call you. When they want you
to die for profit they will let you know.
So, friends, every day do something
that won't compute. Love the Lord.
Love the world. Work for nothing.
Take all that you have and be poor.
Love someone who does not deserve it.
Denounce the government and embrace
the flag. Hope to live in that free
republic for which it stands.
Give your approval to all you cannot
understand. Praise ignorance, for what man
has not encountered he has not destroyed.
Ask the questions that have no answers.
Invest in the millennium. Plant sequoias.

Say that your main crop is the forest
that you did not plant,
that you will not live to harvest.
Say that the leaves are harvested
when they have rotted into the mold.
Call that profit. Prophesy such returns.
Put your faith in the two inches of humus
that will build under the trees
every thousand years.
Listen to carrion—put your ear
close, and hear the faint chattering
of the songs that are to come.
Expect the end of the world. Laugh.
Laughter is immeasurable. Be joyful
though you have considered all the facts.
So long as women do not go cheap
for power, please women more than men.
Ask yourself: Will this satisfy
a woman satisfied to bear a child?
Will this disturb the sleep
of a woman near to giving birth?
Go with your love to the fields.
Lie easy in the shade. Rest your head
in her lap. Swear allegiance
to what is nighest your thoughts.
As soon as the generals and the politicos
can predict the motions of your mind,
lose it. Leave it as a sign
to mark the false trail, the way
you didn't go. Be like the fox
who makes more tracks than necessary,
some in the wrong direction.
Practice resurrection.

A Bookmark

Tom Disch

Four years ago I started reading Proust.
Although I'm past the halfway point, I still
Have seven hundred pages of reduced
Type left before I reach the end. I will
Slog through. It can't get much more dull than what
Is happening now: he's buying crepe-de-chine
Wraps and a real, well-documented hat
For his imaginary Albertine.
Oh, what a slimy sort he must have been—
So weak, so sweetly poisonous, so fey!
Four years ago, by God!—and even then
How I was looking forward to the day
I would be able to forgive, at last,
And to forget *Remembrance of Things Past.*

poetry readings

Charles Bukowski

poetry readings have to be some of the saddest
damned things ever,
the gathering of the clansmen and clanladies,
week after week, month after month, year
after year,
getting old together,
reading on to tiny gatherings,
still hoping their genius will be
discovered,
making tapes together, discs together,
sweating for applause
they read basically to and for
each other,
they can't find a New York publisher
or one
within miles,
but they read on and on
in the poetry holes of America,
never daunted,
never considering the possibility that
their talent might be
thin, almost invisible,
they read on and on
before their mothers, their sisters, their husbands,
their wives, their friends, the other poets

and the handful of idiots who have wandered
in
from nowhere.

I am ashamed for them,
I am ashamed that they have to bolster each other,
I am ashamed for their lisping egos,
their lack of guts.

if these are our creators,
please, please give me something else:

a drunken plumber at a bowling alley,
a prelim boy in a four rounder,
a jock guiding his horse through along the
rail,
a bartender on last call,
a waitress pouring me a coffee,
a drunk sleeping in a deserted doorway,
a dog munching a dry bone,
an elephant's fart in a circus tent,
a 6 p.m. freeway crush,
the mailman telling a dirty joke

anything
anything
but
these.

Emily Dickinson

Publication—is the Auction
Of the Mind of Man—
Poverty—be justifying
For so foul a thing

Possibly—but We—would rather
From Our Garret go
White—Unto the White Creator—
Than invest—Our Snow—

Thought belong to Him who gave it—
Then—to Him Who bear
Its Corporeal illustration—Sell
The Royal Air—

In the Parcel—Be the Merchant
Of the Heavenly Grace—
But reduce no Human Spirit
To Disgrace of Price—

13

TRIPS

Once in the 40s

William Stafford

We were alone one night on a long
road in Montana. This was in winter, a big
night, far to the stars. We had hitched,
my wife and I, and left our ride at
a crossing to go on. Tired and cold—but
brave—we trudged along. This, we said,
was our life, watched over, allowed to go
where we wanted. We said we'd come back some time
when we got rich. We'd leave the others and find
a night like this, whatever we had to give,
and no matter how far, to be so happy again.

from **Moby Dick**

Herman Melville

Call me Ishmael. Some years ago—never mind how long precisely—having little or no money in my purse, and nothing particular to interest me on shore, I thought I would sail about a little and see the watery part of the world. It is a way I have of driving off the spleen and regulating the circulation. Whenever I find myself growing grim about the mouth; whenever it is a damp, drizzly November in my soul; whenever I find myself involuntarily pausing before coffin warehouses, and bringing up the rear of every funeral I meet; and especially whenever my hypos get such an upper hand of me, that it requires a strong moral principle to prevent me from deliberately stepping into the street, and methodically knocking people's hats off—then, I account it high time to get to sea as soon as I can.

Rain Travel

W. S. Merwin

I wake in the dark and remember
it is the morning when I must start
by myself on the journey
I lie listening to the black hour
before dawn and you are
still asleep beside me while
around us the trees full of night lean
hushed in their dream that bears
us up asleep and awake then I hear
drops falling one by one into
the sightless leaves and I
do not know when they began but
all at once there is no sound but rain
and the stream below us roaring
away into the rushing darkness

where we are

Gerald Locklin

(for edward field)

i envy those
who live in two places:
new york, say, and london;
wales and spain;
l.a. and paris;
hawaii and switzerland.

there is always the anticipation
of the change, the chance that what is wrong
is the result of where you are. i have
always loved both the freshness of
arriving and the relief of leaving. with
two homes every move would be a homecoming.
i am not even considering the weather, hot
or cold, dry or wet: i am talking about hope.

Excelsior

Henry Wadsworth Longfellow

The shades of night were falling fast,
As through an Alpine village passed
A youth, who bore, 'mid snow and ice,
A banner with the strange device,
     Excelsior!

His brow was sad; his eye beneath
Flashed like a falchion from its sheath,
And like a silver clarion rung
The accents of that unknown tongue,
     Excelsior!

In happy homes he saw the light
Of household fires gleam warm and bright;
Above, the spectral glaciers shone,
And from his lips escaped a groan,
     Excelsior!

"Try not the Pass!" the old man said;
"Dark lowers the tempest overhead,
The roaring torrent is deep and wide!"
And loud that clarion voice replied,
     Excelsior!

"Oh stay," the maiden said, "and rest
Thy weary head upon this breast!"
A tear stood in his bright blue eye,
But still he answered, with a sigh,
      Excelsior!

"Beware the pine-tree's withered branch!
Beware the awful avalanche!"
This was the peasant's last Good-night,
A voice replied, far up the height,
      Excelsior!

At break of day, as heavenward
The pious monks of St. Bernard
Uttered the oft-repeated prayer,
A voice cried through the startled air,
      Excelsior!

A traveller, by the faithful hound,
Half-buried in the snow was found,
Still grasping in his hand of ice
That banner with the strange device,
      Excelsior!

There in the twilight cold and gray,
Lifeless, but beautiful, he lay,
And from the sky, serene and far,
A voice fell, like a falling star,
      Excelsior!

On a Tree Fallen Across the Road
(To Hear Us Talk)

Robert Frost

The tree the tempest with a crash of wood
Throws down in front of us is not to bar
Our passage to our journey's end for good,
But just to ask us who we think we are

Insisting always on our own way so.
She likes to halt us in our runner tracks,
And make us get down in a foot of snow
Debating what to do without an axe.

And yet she knows obstruction is in vain:
We will not be put off the final goal
We have it hidden in us to attain,
Not though we have to seize earth by the pole

And, tired of aimless circling in one place,
Steer straight off after something into space.

A Walk Along the Old Tracks

Robert Kinsley

When I was young they had already been
abandoned for years
overgrown with sumac and sour apple,
the iron scrapped, the wood long
gone for other things.
In summer my father would send us along them
to fetch the cows from the back pasture,
a long walk to a far off place it seemed
for boys so young. Lost again for a moment
in that simple place,
I fling apples from a stick and look for snakes
in the gullies. There is
a music to the past, the sweet tones
of perfect octaves
even though we know it was never so.
My father had to sell the farm in that near perfect time
and once old Al Shott killed a six foot rattler on the tracks.
"And when the trolly was running" he said, "you could jump
her as she went by and ride all the way to Cleveland,
and oh," he said, "what a time you could have there."

Passengers

Billy Collins

At the gate, I sit in a row of blue seats
with the possible company of my death,
this sprawling miscellany of people—
carry-on bags and paperbacks—

that could be gathered in a flash
into a band of pilgrims on the last open road.
Not that I think
if our plane crumpled into a mountain

we would all ascend together,
holding hands like a ring of skydivers,
into a sudden gasp of brightness,
or that there would be some common place

for us to reunite to jubilize the moment,
some spaceless, pillarless Greece
where we could, at the count of three,
toss our ashes into the sunny air.

It's just that the way that man has his briefcase
so carefully arranged,
the way that girl is cooling her tea,
and the flow of the comb that woman

passes through her daughter's hair . . .
and when you consider the altitude,
the secret parts of the engines,
and all the hard water and the deep canyons below . . .

well, I just think it would be good if one of us
maybe stood up and said a few words,
or, so as not to involve the police,
at least quietly wrote something down.

The Walloping Window-Blind

Charles Edward Carryl

A capital ship for an ocean trip
    Was *The Walloping Window-blind*—
No gale that blew dismayed her crew
    Or troubled the captain's mind.
The man at the wheel was taught to feel
    Contempt for the wildest blow,
And it often appeared, when the weather had cleared,
    That he'd been in his bunk below.

The boatswain's mate was very sedate,
    Yet fond of amusement, too;
And he played hop-scotch with the starboard watch,
    While the captain tickled the crew.
And the gunner we had was apparently mad,
    For he sat on the after-rail,
And fired salutes with the captain's boots,
    In the teeth of the booming gale.

The captain sat in a commodore's hat
    And dined, in a royal way,
On toasted pigs and pickles and figs
    And gummery bread, each day.
But the cook was Dutch, and behaved as such;
    For the food that he gave the crew
Was a number of tons of hot-cross buns,
    Chopped up with sugar and glue.

And we all felt ill as mariners will,
    On a diet that's cheap and rude;
And we shivered and shook as we dipped the cook
    In a tub of his gluesome food.
Then nautical pride we laid aside,
    And we cast the vessel ashore
On the Gulliby Isles, where the Poohpooh smiles,
    And the Anagazanders roar.

Composed of sand was that favored land,
    And trimmed with cinnamon straws;
And pink and blue was the pleasing hue
    Of the Tickletoeteaser's claws.
And we sat on the edge of a sandy ledge
    And shot at the whistling bee;
And the Binnacle-bats wore water-proof hats
    As they danced in the sounding sea.

On rubagub bark, from dawn to dark,
    We fed, till we all had grown
Uncommonly shrunk,—when a Chinese junk
    Came by from the torriby zone.
She was stubby and square, but we didn't much care,
    And we cheerily put to sea;
And we left the crew of the junk to chew
    The bark of the rubagub tree.

The Vacation

Wendell Berry

Once there was a man who filmed his vacation.
He went flying down the river in his boat
with his video camera to his eye, making
a moving picture of the moving river
upon which his sleek boat moved swiftly
toward the end of his vacation. He showed
his vacation to his camera, which pictured it,
preserving it forever: the river, the trees,
the sky, the light, the bow of his rushing boat
behind which he stood with his camera
preserving his vacation even as he was having it
so that after he had had it he would still
have it. It would be there. With a flick
of a switch, there it would be. But he
would not be in it. He would never be in it.

Directions

Joseph Stroud

How weary, stale, flat, and unprofitable
Seem to me all the uses of this world

Take a plane to London.
From King's Cross take the direct train to York.
Rent a car and drive across the vale to Ripon,
then into the dales toward the valley of the Nidd,
a narrow road with high stone walls on each side,
and soon you'll be on the moors. There's a pub,
The Drovers, where it's warm inside, a tiny room,
you can stand at the counter and drink a pint of Old Peculiar.
For a moment everything will be all right. You're back
at a beginning. Soon you'll walk into Yorkshire country,
into dells, farms, into blackberry and cloud country.
You'll walk for hours. You'll walk the freshness
back into your life. This is true. You can do this.
Even now, sitting at your desk, worrying, troubled,
you can gaze across Middlesmoor to Ramsgill,
the copses, the abbeys of slanting light, the fells,
you can look down on that figure walking toward Scar House,
cheeks flushed, curlews rising in front of him, walking,
making his way, working his life, step by step, into grace.

Postscript

Seamus Heaney

And some time make the time to drive out west
Into County Clare, along the Flaggy Shore,
In September or October, when the wind
And the light are working off each other
So that the ocean on one side is wild
With foam and glitter, and inland among stones
The surface of a slate-grey lake is lit
By the earthed lightning of a flock of swans,
Their feathers roughed and ruffling, white on white,
Their fully grown headstrong-looking heads
Tucked or cresting or busy underwater.
Useless to think you'll park and capture it
More thoroughly. You are neither here nor there,
A hurry through which known and strange things pass
As big soft buffetings come at the car sideways
And catch the heart off guard and blow it open.

Night Journey

Theodore Roethke

Now as the train bears west,
Its rhythm rocks the earth,
And from my Pullman berth
I stare into the night
While others take their rest.
Bridges of iron lace,
A suddenness of trees,
A lap of mountain mist
All cross my line of sight,
Then a bleak wasted place,
And a lake below my knees.
Full on my neck I feel
The straining at a curve;
My muscles move with steel,
I wake in every nerve.
I watch a beacon swing
From dark to blazing bright;
We thunder through ravines
And gullies washed with light.
Beyond the mountain pass
Mist deepens on the pane;
We rush into a rain
That rattles double glass.
Wheels shake the roadbed stone,
The pistons jerk and shove,
I stay up half the night
To see the land I love.

Waiting

Raymond Carver

Left off the highway and
down the hill. At the
bottom, hang another left.
Keep bearing left. The road
will make a Y. Left again.
There's a creek on the left.
Keep going. Just before
the road ends, there'll be
another road. Take it
and no other. Otherwise,
your life will be ruined
forever. There's a log house
with a shake roof, on the left.
It's not that house. It's
the next house, just over
a rise. The house
where trees are laden with
fruit. Where phlox, forsythia,
and marigold grow. It's
the house where the woman
stands in the doorway
wearing sun in her hair. The one
who's been waiting
all this time.
The woman who loves you.
The one who can say,
"What's kept you?"

14

SNOW

New Hampshire

Howard Moss

1
When the loons cry,
The night seems blacker,
The water deeper.

Across the shore:
An eyelash-charcoal
Fringe of pine trees.

2
The lake reflects
Indefinite pewter,

And intermittent thunder
Lets us know

The gods are arriving,
One valley over.

3
After the long
Melancholy of the fall,
One longs for the crisp
Brass shout of winter—

The blaze of firewood,
The window's spill
Of parlor lamplight
Across the snow.

4
Flaring like a match
Dropped in a dry patch,
One sunset tells
The spectrum's story.

See the last hunter's
Flashlight dim
As he hurries home
To his lighted window.

Emily Dickinson

To fight aloud, is very brave—
But *gallanter*, I know
Who charge within the bosom
The Cavalry of Woe—

Who win, and nations do not see—
Who fall—and none observe—
Whose dying eyes, no Country
Regards with patriot love—

We trust, in plumed procession
For such, the Angels go—
Rank after Rank, with even feet—
And Uniforms of Snow.

December Moon

May Sarton

Before going to bed
After a fall of snow
I look out on the field
Shining there in the moonlight
So calm, untouched and white
Snow silence fills my head
After I leave the window.

Hours later near dawn
When I look down again
The whole landscape has changed
The perfect surface gone
Criss-crossed and written on
Where the wild creatures ranged
While the moon rose and shone.

Why did my dog not bark?
Why did I hear no sound
There on the snow-locked ground
In the tumultuous dark?

How much can come, how much can go
When the December moon is bright,
What worlds of play we'll never know
Sleeping away the cold white night
After a fall of snow.

Year's End

Richard Wilbur

Now winter downs the dying of the year,
And night is all a settlement of snow;
From the soft street the rooms of houses show
A gathered light, a shapen atmosphere,
Like frozen-over lakes whose ice is thin
And still allows some stirring down within.

I've known the wind by water banks to shake
The late leaves down, which frozen where they fell
And held in ice as dancers in a spell
Fluttered all winter long into a lake;
Graved on the dark in gestures of descent,
They seemed their own most perfect monument.

There was perfection in the death of ferns
Which laid their fragile cheeks against the stone
A million years. Great mammoths overthrown
Composedly have made their long sojourns,
Like palaces of patience, in the gray
And changeless lands of ice. And at Pompeii

The little dog lay curled and did not rise
But slept the deeper as the ashes rose
And found the people incomplete, and froze
The random hands, the loose unready eyes

Of men expecting yet another sun
To do the shapely thing they had not done.

These sudden ends of time must give us pause.
We fray into the future, rarely wrought
Save in the tapestries of afterthought.
More time, more time. Barrages of applause
Come muffled from a buried radio.
The New-year bells are wrangling with the snow.

The Snow Man

Wallace Stevens

One must have a mind of winter
To regard the frost and the boughs
Of the pine-trees crusted with snow;

And have been cold a long time
To behold the junipers shagged with ice,
The spruces rough in the distant glitter

Of the January sun; and not to think
Of any misery in the sound of the wind,
In the sound of a few leaves,

Which is the sound of the land
Full of the same wind
That is blowing in the same bare place

For the listener, who listens in the snow,
And, nothing himself, beholds
Nothing that is not there and the nothing that is.

January

Baron Wormser

"Cold as the moon," he'd mutter
In the January of 5 A.M. and 15 below
As he tried to tease the old Chev into greeting
One more misanthropic morning.

It was an art (though he never
Used that curious word) as he thumped
The gas pedal and turned the key
So carefully while he held his breath
And waited for the sharp jounce
And roar of an engaged engine.

"Shoulda brought in the battery last night."
"Shoulda got up around midnight
And turned it over once."

It was always early rising as he'd worked
A lifetime "in every damn sort
Of damn factory." Machines were
As natural to him as dogs and flowers.
A machine, as he put it, "was sensible."

I was so stupid about valves and intakes
He thought I was some religious type.
How had I lived as long as I had
And remained so out of it?

And why had I moved of my own free will
To a place that prided itself
On the blunt misery of January?

"No way to live," he'd say as he poked
A finger into the frozen throat
Of an unwilling carburetor.
His breath hung in the air
Like a white balloon.

Later on the way to the town where
We worked while the heater
Wheezed fitfully and the windshield
Showed indifference to the defroster
He'd turn to me and say that
The two best things in this world
Were hot coffee and winter sunrises.
The icy road beckoned to no one,
Snow began to drift down sleepily,
The peace of servitude sighed and dreamed.

in celebration of surviving

Chuck Miller

when senselessness has pounded you around on the ropes
and you're getting too old to hold out for the future
no work and running out of money,
and then you make a try after something that you know you
    won't get
and this long shot comes through on the stretch
in a photo finish of your heart's trepidation
then for a while
even when the chill factor of these prairie winters puts it at
    fifty below
you're warm and have that old feeling
of being a comer, though belated
in the crazy game of life

standing in the winter night
emptying the garbage and looking at the stars
you realize that although the odds are fantastically against you
when that single January shooting star
flung its wad in the maw of night
it was yours
and though the years are edged with crime and squalor
that second wind, or twenty-third
is coming strong
and for a time
perhaps a very short time
one lives as though in a golden envelope of light

Her Long Illness

Donald Hall

Daybreak until nightfall,
he sat by his wife at the hospital
    while chemotherapy dripped
through the catheter into her heart.
    He drank coffee and read
the *Globe.* He paced; he worked
    on poems; he rubbed her back
and read aloud. Overcome with dread,
    they wept and affirmed
their love for each other, witlessly,
    over and over again.
When it snowed one morning Jane gazed
    at the darkness blurred
with flakes. They pushed the IV pump
    which she called Igor
slowly past the nurses' pods, as far
    as the outside door
so that she could smell the snowy air.

Requiescat

Oscar Wilde

Tread lightly, she is near
    Under the snow,
Speak gently, she can hear
    The daisies grow.

All her bright golden hair
    Tarnished with rust,
She that was young and fair
    Fallen to dust.

Lily-like, white as snow,
    She hardly knew
She was a woman, so
    Sweetly she grew.

Coffin-board, heavy stone,
    Lie on her breast,
I vex my heart alone
    She is at rest.

Peace, peace, she cannot hear
    Lyre or sonnet,
All my life's buried here,
    Heap earth upon it.

The Sixth of January

David Budbill

The cat sits on the back of the sofa looking
out the window through the softly falling snow
at the last bit of gray light.

I can't say the sun is going down.
We haven't seen the sun for two months.
Who cares?

I am sitting in the blue chair listening to this stillness.
The only sound: the occasional gurgle of tea
coming out of the pot and into the cup.

How can this be?
Such calm, such peace, such solitude
in this world of woe.

Not Only the Eskimos

Lisel Mueller

We have only one noun
but as many different kinds:

the grainy snow of the Puritans
and snow of soft, fat flakes,

guerrilla snow, which comes in the night
and changes the world by morning,

rabbinical snow, a permanent skullcap
on the highest mountains,

snow that blows in like the Lone Ranger,
riding hard from out of the West,

surreal snow in the Dakotas,
when you can't find your house, your street,
though you are not in a dream
or a science-fiction movie,

snow that tastes good to the sun
when it licks black tree limbs,
leaving us only one white stripe,
a replica of a skunk,

unbelievable snows:
the blizzard that strikes on the tenth of April,
the false snow before Indian summer
the Big Snow on Mozart's birthday,
when Chicago became the Elysian Fields
and strangers spoke to each other,

paper snow, cut and taped
to the inside of grade-school windows,

in an old tale, the snow
that covers a nest of strawberries,
small hearts, ripe and sweet,

the special snow that goes with Christmas,
whether it falls or not,

the Russian snow we remember
along with the warmth and smell of our furs,
though we have never traveled
to Russia or worn furs,

Villon's snows of yesteryear,
lost with ladies gone out like matches,
the snow in Joyce's "The Dead,"
the silent, secret snow
in a story by Conrad Aiken,
which is the snow of first love,

the snowfall between the child
and the spacewoman on TV,

snow as idea of whiteness,
as in *snowdrop, snow goose, snowball bush*,

the snow that puts stars in your hair,
and your hair, which has turned to snow,

the snow Elinor Wylie walked in
in velvet shoes,

the snow before her footprints
and the snow after,

the snow in the back of our heads,
whiter than white, which has to do
with childhood again each year.

Boy at the Window

Richard Wilbur

Seeing the snowman standing all alone
In the dusk and cold is more than he can bear.
The small boy weeps to hear the wind prepare
A night of gnashings and enormous moan.
His tearful sight can hardly reach to where
The pale-faced figure with bitumen eyes
Returns him such a god-forsaken stare
As outcast Adam gave to Paradise.

The man of snow is, nonetheless, content,
Having no wish to go inside and die.
Still, he is moved to see the youngster cry.
Though frozen water is his element,
He melts enough to drop from one soft eye
A trickle of the purest rain, a tear
For the child at the bright pane surrounded by
Such warmth, such light, such love, and so much fear.

Winter Poem

Frederick Morgan

We made love on a winter afternoon
and when we woke, hours had turned and changed,
the moon was shining, and the earth was new.
The city, with its lines and squares, was gone:
our room had placed itself on a small hill
surrounded by dark woods frosted in snow
and meadows where the flawless drifts lay deep.
No men there—some small animals all fur
stared gently at us with soft-shining eyes
as we stared back through the chill frosty panes.
Absolute cold gave us our warmth that night,
we held hands in the pure throes of delight,
the air we breathed was washed clean by the snow.

Lester Tells of Wanda and the Big Snow

Paul Zimmer

Some years back I worked a strip mine
Out near Tylersburg. One day it starts
To snow and by two we got three feet.
I says to the foreman, "I'm going home."
He says, "Ain't you stayin' till five?"
I says, "I got to see to my cows,"
Not telling how Wanda was there at the house.
By the time I make it home at four
Another foot is down and it don't quit
Until it lays another. Wanda and me
For three whole days seen no one else.
We tunneled the drifts and slid
Right over the barbed wire, laughing
At how our heartbeats melted the snow.
After a time the food was gone and I thought
I'd butcher a cow, but then it cleared
And the moon come up as sweet as an apple.
Next morning the ploughs got through. It made us sad.
It don't snow like that no more. Too bad.

Old Boards

Robert Bly

I
I love to see boards lying on the ground in early spring:
The ground beneath them is wet, and muddy—
Perhaps covered with chicken tracks—
And they are dry and eternal.

II
This is the wood one sees on the decks of ocean ships,
Wood that carries us far from land,
With a dryness of something used for simple tasks,
Like a horse's tail.

III
This wood is like a man who has a simple life,
Living through the spring and winter on the ship of his own
    desire.
He sits on dry wood surrounded by half-melted snow
As the rooster walks away springily over the dampened hay.

March Blizzard

John Tagliabue

A thin and crippled and sweet and humorous
very old man dying, on his winter bed,
in an oxygen tent, very very thin, Irish,
such a good Yankee craftsman, ascetic,
bachelor, dreamy philosophic; a few weeks ago
he climbed a thin ladder to take some snow
and ice off the roof, boyish up there he worked,
clear; now in the painted hospital he tries
to breathe; the whole wide day is dim
with heavy snow, it is still snowing; a dying
whale in the vast sea comes up several times
for air; what angels are ready?

                And *then*
fooling all the predictions of the doctors and charts
and tremulous fears of his brother and sisters
(they adore him, and one had a permanent-wave
just to be ready in case)—and then he came out
of the hospital, went down to the grocery store
to see some friends; and recently
                      he's been on
                      the roof again!

15

YELLOW

Elvis Kissed Me

T. S. Kerrigan

"Elvis kissed me once," she swears,
sitting in a neon dive
ordering her drinks in pairs.

Two stools down you nurse a beer,
sensing easy pickings here.

"Back in sixty-eight," she sighs,
smoothing back her yellow hair.
Teared mascara smears her eyes.

Drawing near, you claim you've met,
offer her a cigarette.

"Call me cheap," she sobs, "or bad,
say that decent men dismissed me,
say I've lost my looks, but add,
Elvis kissed me."

Stepping Out of Poetry

Gerald Stern

What would you give for one of the old yellow streetcars
rocking toward you again through the thick snow?

What would you give for the feeling of joy as you climbed
up the three iron steps and took your place by the cold window?

Oh, what would you give to pick up your stack of books
and walk down the icy path in front of the library?

What would you give for your dream
to be as clear and simple as it was then
in the dark afternoons, at the old scarred tables?

Emily Dickinson

I shall keep singing!
Birds will pass me
On their way to Yellower Climes—
Each—with a Robin's expectation—
I—with my Redbreast—
And my Rhymes—

Late—when I take my place in summer—
But—I shall bring a fuller tune—
Vespers—are sweeter than Matins—Signor—
Morning—only the seed of Noon—

Song to Onions

Roy Blount, Jr.

They improve everything, pork chops to soup,
And not only that but each onion's a group.

Peel back the skin, delve into tissue
And see how an onion has been blessed with issue.

Every layer produces an ovum:
You think you've got three then you find you've got fovum.

Onion on on-
Ion on onion they run,
Each but the smallest one some onion's mother:
An onion comprises a half-dozen other.

In sum then an onion you could say is less
Than the sum of its parts.
But then I like things that more are than profess—
In food and in the arts.

Things pungent, not tony.
I'll take Damon Runyon
Over Antonioni—
Who if an *i* wanders becomes Anti-onion.
I'm anti-baloney.

Although a baloney sandwich would
Right now, with onions, be right good.

And so would sliced onions,
              Chewed with cheese,
Or onions chopped and sprinkled
              Over black-eyed peas:

  Black-eyed,
    grey-gravied,
        absorbent of essences,
            eaten on New Year's Eve
            peas.

O Luxury

Guy W. Longchamps

O what a luxury it be
how exquisite, what perfect bliss
so ordinary and yet chic
to pee to piss to take a leak

To feel your bladder just go free
and open like the Mighty Miss
and all your cares go down the creek
to pee to piss to take a leak

for gentlemen of great physique
who can hold water for one week
for ladies who one-quarter cup
of tea can fill completely up
for folks in urinalysis
for Viennese and Greek and Swiss
for little kids just learning this
for everyone it's pretty great
to urinate
women are quite circumspect
but men can piss with great effect
with terrible hydraulic force
can make a stream or change its course
can put out fires or cigarettes
and sometimes
laying down our bets

late at night outside the bars
we like to aim up at the stars.

Yes for men it's much more grand
women sit or squat
we stand
and hold the fellow in our hand
and proudly watch the yellow arc
adjust the range and make our mark
on stones and posts for rival men
to smell and not come back again

Coming

Kenneth Rexroth

You are driving to the airport
Along the glittering highway
Through the warm night,
Humming to yourself.
The yellow rose buds that stood
On the commode faded and fell
Two days ago. Last night the
Petals dropped from the tulips
On the dresser. The signs of
Your presence are leaving the
House one by one. Being without
You was almost more than I
Could bear. Now the work is squared
Away. All the arrangements
Have been made. All the delays
Are past and I am thirty
Thousand feet in the air over
A dark lustrous sea, under
A low half moon that makes the wings
Gleam like a fish under water—
Rushing south four hundred miles
Down the California coast
To your curving lips and your
Ivory thighs.

A Light Left On

May Sarton

In the evening we came back
Into our yellow room,
For a moment taken aback
To find the light left on,
Falling on silent flowers,
Table, book, empty chair
While we had gone elsewhere,
Had been away for hours.

When we came home together
We found the inside weather.
All of our love unended
The quiet light demanded,
And we gave, in a look
At yellow walls and open book.
The deepest world we share
And do not talk about
But have to have, was there,
And by that light found out.

The Yellow Slicker

Stuart Dischell

On this fourth day in a row of rain
There is a sameness to the streets broken only by the odd
Brightly painted house—the way those who pass by
In tan or black trench coats look back at the girl
Wearing a yellow slicker. The yellow slicker,
A gift from her aunt who knew London would be wet,
Having lived there herself just after The War,
The Europe she had known transformed to a state
Of the mind, no longer Central but Eastern, far away,
Bombed-out, depopulated, at least of her kind.

But for a girl of nineteen with American thoughts,
Traveler's cheques, a boy at home, a university
Address, the decline of the West compels less
Than each step she takes through the London rain.
Even these British so accustomed to their weather
Admire the girl in the yellow slicker, as if she
With her uncovered streaming blond hair might shine
As the only sun they will see all week. Now,
That's the kind of history she likes to hear.

First Kiss

April Lindner

This collision of teeth, of tongues and lips,
is like feeling for the door
in a strange room, blindfolded.
He imagines he knows her
after four dates, both of them taking pains
to laugh correctly, to make eye contact.
She thinks at least this long first kiss
postpones the moment she'll have to face
four white walls, the kitchen table,
its bowl of dry petals and nutmeg husks,
the jaunty yellow vase with one jaunty bloom,
the answering machine's one bloodshot eye.

The Music One Looks Back On

Stephen Dobyns

In early autumn, there's a concerto
possible when there's a guest in the house
and the guest is taking a shower and the host
is washing up from the night before.
With each turn of the tap in the kitchen,
the water temperature increases or drops
upstairs and the guest responds with little groans—
cold water for low notes, hot water for high.
His hair is soapy, the tub slippery
and with his groaning he becomes the concerto's
primary instrument. Then let's say the night
was particularly frosty and now the radiators
are knocking, filling the house with warmth,
and the children are rushing around outside
in the leaves before breakfast, calling after
their Irish setter whose name is Cleveland.
And still asleep, the host's wife is making
those little sighs one makes before waking,
as she turns and resettles and the bed creaks.
Standing at the sink, the host hums to himself
as he thinks of the eggs he'll soon fry up,
while already there's the crackle of bacon
from the stove and a smell of coffee. The mild groans
of the guest, the radiator's percussion,
children's high voices, the barking of a dog,
even the wife's small sighs and resettlings

combine into this autumn concerto of which
not one of the musicians is aware as they drift
toward breakfast and then a leisurely walk
through the fields near the house—two friends
who haven't seen each other for over a year.
Much later they will remember only a color,
a golden yellow, and the sound of their feet
scuffling the leaves. A day without rancor
or angry words, the sort of day that builds a life,
becoming a soft place to look back on,
and geese, geese flying south out of winter.

16

LIVES

In a Prominent Bar in Secaucus One Day

X. J. Kennedy

In a prominent bar in Secaucus one day
Rose a lady in skunk with a topheavy sway,
Raised a knobby red finger—all turned from their beer—
While with eyes bright as snowcrust she sang high and clear:

"Now who of you'd think from an eyeload of me
That I once was a lady as proud as could be?
Oh I'd never sit down by a tumbledown drunk
If it wasn't, my dears, for the high cost of junk.

"All the gents used to swear that the white of my calf
Beat the down of the swan by a length and a half.
In the kerchief of linen I caught to my nose
Ah, there never fell snot, but a little gold rose.

"I had seven gold teeth and a toothpick of gold,
My Virginia cheroot was a leaf of it rolled
And I'd light it each time with a thousand in cash—
Why the bums used to fight if I flicked them an ash.

"Once the toast of the Biltmore, the belle of the Taft,
I would drink bottle beer at the Drake, never draft,
And dine at the Astor on Salisbury steak
With a clean tablecloth for each bite I did take.

"In a car like the Roxy I'd roll to the track,
A steel-guitar trio, a bar in the back,
And the wheels made no noise, they turned over so fast,
Still it took you ten minutes to see me go past.

"When the horses bowed down to me that I might choose,
I bet on them all, for I hated to lose.
Now I'm saddled each night for my butter and eggs
And the broken threads race down the backs of my legs.

"Let you hold in mind, girls, that your beauty must pass
Like a lovely white clover that rusts with its grass.
Keep your bottoms off barstools and marry you young
Or be left—an old barrel with many a bung.

"For when time takes you out for a spin in his car
You'll be hard-pressed to stop him from going too far
And be left by the roadside, for all your good deeds,
Two toadstools for tits and a face full of weeds."

All the house raised a cheer, but the man at the bar
Made a phonecall and up pulled a red patrol car
And she blew us a kiss as they copped her away
From that prominent bar in Secaucus, N.J.

Who's Who

W. H. Auden

A shilling life will give you all the facts:
How Father beat him, how he ran away,
What were the struggles of his youth, what acts
Made him the greatest figure of his day:
Of how he fought, fished, hunted, worked all night,
Though giddy, climbed new mountains; named a sea:
Some of the last researchers even write
Love made him weep his pints like you and me.

With all his honours on, he sighed for one
Who, say astonished critics, lived at home;
Did little jobs about the house with skill
And nothing else; could whistle; would sit still
Or potter round the garden; answered some
Of his long marvellous letters but kept none.

The Portrait

Stanley Kunitz

My mother never forgave my father
for killing himself,
especially at such an awkward time
and in a public park,
that spring
when I was waiting to be born.
She locked his name
in her deepest cabinet
and would not let him out,
though I could hear him thumping.
When I came down from the attic
with the pastel portrait in my hand
of a long-lipped stranger
with a brave moustache
and deep brown level eyes,
she ripped it into shreds
without a single word
and slapped me hard.
In my sixty-fourth year
I can feel my cheek
still burning.

Parable of the Four-Poster

Erica Jong

Because she wants to touch him,
she moves away.
Because she wants to talk to him,
she keeps silent.
Because she wants to kiss him,
she turns away
& kisses a man she does not want to kiss.

He watches
thinking she does not want him.
He listens
hearing her silence.
He turns away
thinking her distant
& kisses a girl he does not want to kiss.

They marry each other—
a four-way mistake.
He goes to bed with his wife
thinking of her.
She goes to bed with her husband
thinking of him.
—& all this in a real old-fashioned four-poster bed.

Do they live unhappily ever after?
Of course.
Do they undo their mistakes ever?
Never.
Who is the victim here?
Love is the victim.
Who is the villain?
Love that never dies.

Ed

Louis Simpson

Ed was in love with a cocktail waitress,
but Ed's family, and his friends,
didn't approve. So he broke it off.

He married a respectable woman
who played the piano. She played well enough
to have been a professional.

Ed's wife left him . . .
Years later, at a family gathering
Ed got drunk and made a fool of himself.

He said, "I should have married Doreen."
"Well," they said, "why didn't you?"

Memory

Hayden Carruth

A woman I used to know well died
      A week ago. Not to be mysterious:
She and I were married. I'm told
      She fell down dead on a street in
Lower Manhattan, and I suppose
      She suffered a stroke or a heart attack.
The last time I saw her was in the spring
      Of 1955, meaning forty-four
Years ago, and now when I try
      To imagine her death I see in my
Mind a good-looking, twenty-nine-
      Year-old woman sprawled on the pavement.
It does no good to go and examine
      My own ravaged face in the bathroom
Mirror; I cannot transpose my ravage-
      Ment to her. She is fixed in my mind
As she was. Brown hair, brown eyes,
      Slender and sexy, coming home
From her job as an editor in a huge
      Building in midtown. Forty-four
Years is longer than I thought. My dear,
      How could you have let this happen to you?

Lazy

David Lee

Laziest man ever was Floyd Scott
it wasn't nothing that boy
would ever do for anybody
when he's 5 years old
arredy too late his mama one day
sez Floyd come take this trash out
to the barrel but he just lain there
in the living room on the furniture
so she sez you taking this trash out
like I told you?
he never answered she sed
you want to take this trash out
to the barrel or do you want a whipping?
he sez finally how many licks?
she sed 3 with the flyswatter
he didn't say nothing for a minute
she thought he's coming to get it
then he sed do I have to
come out there or will you come
give it to me in here? . . .

. . . he was 24 years old when he
went and got in the car to drive
down to the grocery store a block away
to get him a can of beer
had this terrible itch that was a tragedy

he stretched up to scratch his ast
hit the curb and rolled the car
on flat ground right over
Doctor sed he couldn't find
nothing wrong with the x-ray
but his back wasn't strong enough
for him to walk on it after that
insurance bought him 4 different wheelchairs
all too hard for him to use
till they got one with a electric motor on it
he sed he was satisfied
never walked a hundred steps in a row after that
some days he sed it was too hard and not worth the effort
to even get out of bed to it
so he got a television set in his bedroom
to help him get by on social security
that same year 4 kinds of welfare
and the Assemblyofgod brought his supper
on all days with a R in them

county paid for him a private nurse
because he sed it was a soft spot
in that pavement caused his accident
of their negligence and behavior
he was gone sue the county
and the town for a million dollars
if they didn't take care of him till he got well
they thought it'd be cheaper to buy him a nurse
for however long it took
after 3 years she found a way to get married to him
and still have the county pay her for being a nurse's helper
bought them a trailerhouse they put in
right next to his daddy's house

where he didn't have to pay no rent
after that she give up her other patients
and kept the county money for watching him
it was enough to get by on they sed

she's almost as lazy as he was
I heard moss grown in her toilets
they put a deep freezer out on the front porch
to hold the TV dinners she fixed
on all days without a R
both of them got so fat they had to have 2 couches
in the living room to set and watch TV on
so lazy a dog couldn't live with them
it'd of starved to death waiting
for one of them to come feed it

Testimonial

Harry Newman, Jr.

You are cordially invited
To attend, at $100 a plate
A testimonial to those
Who have devoted their lives
Unstintingly
Unselfishly
To the humanitarian purpose
Of making money.

No sacrifice too great
No relationship too dear
To accumulate enough
To afford the luxury

Of giving it away
In some worthy cause
Or other.

Just listen to that applause
From the thousand or more
Gathered here in tribute,
Black tied, bejeweled,
Pledging their allegiance
To the honorees and
To the secret hope

That one such memorable night
They too might step
Into the blue-white shaft
And receive their plaque.

Cathedral Builders

John Ormond

They climbed on sketchy ladders towards God,
With winch and pulley hoisted hewn rock into heaven,
Inhabited sky with hammers, defied gravity,
Deified stone, took up God's house to meet Him,

And came down to their suppers and small beer;
Every night slept, lay with their smelly wives,
Quarrelled and cuffed the children, lied,
Spat, sang, were happy or unhappy,

And every day took to the ladders again;
Impeded the rights of way of another summer's
Swallows, grew greyer, shakier, became less inclined
To fix a neighbour's roof of a fine evening,

Saw naves sprout arches, clerestories soar,
Cursed the loud fancy glaziers for their luck,
Somehow escaped the plague, got rheumatism,
Decided it was time to give it up,

To leave the spire to others; stood in the crowd
Well back from the vestments at the consecration,
Envied the fat bishop his warm boots,
Cocked up a squint eye and said, "I bloody did that."

The Village Burglar

Anonymous

Under the spreading gooseberry bush
    The village burglar lies;
The burglar is a hairy man
    With whiskers round his eyes.

He goes to church on Sundays;
    He hears the Parson shout;
He puts a penny in the plate
    And takes a shilling out

The Scandal

Robert Bly

The day the minister ran off with the choir director
The bindlestiffs felt some gaiety in their arms.
Spike-pitchers threw their bundles higher on the load
And the County Assessor drove with a tiny smile.

Actually the minister's wife felt relieved that
    morning,
Though afraid too. She walked out by the slough,
And admired the beaver's house, partly above
Water, partly beneath. That seemed right.

The minister felt dizzy as the two of them drove
For hours: country music and the loose ribbon
Mingled in his mind with the *Song of Songs*.
They stopped at a small motel near Bismarck.

For the threshers, the stubble was still dry,
The oat dust itchy, the big belt needed grease,
The loads pulled up to the machine. This story
    happens
Over and over, and it's a good story.

At Last the Secret Is Out

W. H. Auden

At last the secret is out, as it always must come in the end,
The delicious story is ripe to tell to the intimate friend;
Over the tea-cups and in the square the tongue has its desire;
Still waters run deep, my dear, there's never smoke without fire.

Behind the corpse in the reservoir, behind the ghost on the links,
Behind the lady who dances and the man who madly drinks,
Under the look of fatigue, the attack of migraine and the sigh
There is always another story, there is more than meets the eye.

For the clear voice suddenly singing, high up in the convent wall,
The scent of the elder bushes, the sporting prints in the hall,
The croquet matches in summer, the handshake, the cough, the
    kiss,
There is always a wicked secret, a private reason for this.

Night Light

Kate Barnes

Lying in bed in the pitch black, a little breathing
    underlies my own;
it is my dog on the floor; we are both alive here.
And I struggle with the old illusion; there is
    something else in the room,
a story in the darkness—if I wake up I can
    write it down.
It is the light of the purple grape, the deep glowing light
that emanates from my black horse's flank, the knee-
    length, straight,
shiny black hair of the round-faced girl in Sonora
dancing with her groom at the fiesta while all the
    aunts sat and smiled;
or it is the telephone pole with *Black Beauty* stamped
    on it, or the thin black dog
named Ink Spot, or the one sleek all-black cow with black
    horns—
in the herd of Holsteins always a silhouette; it is the
    screaming games
of murder in the dark house, the quick uncertain
    kiss in the pantry, the running feet;
they are all here in the darkness with me, they crowd
    me with their light.

Sir Patrick Spens

Anonymous

The king sits in Dumferlin town
    Drinking the blood-red wine:
Oh where will I get a good sailor
    To sail this ship of mine?

Up and spake an eldern knight
    Sat at the king's right knee:
Sir Patrick Spens is the best sailor
    That sails upon the sea.

The king has written a broad letter
    And signed it with his hand,
And sent it to Sir Patrick Spens
    Was walking on the strand.

To Noroway, to Noroway,
    To Noroway o'er the foam,
The king's daughter to Noroway,
    'Tis thou maun bring her home.

The first line that Sir Patrick read
    A loud laugh laughed he;
The next line that Sir Patrick read
    A tear blinded his eye.

Oh who is this has done this deed,
    This ill deed done to me,
To send me out this time of the year
    To sail upon the sea?

Make haste, make haste, my merry men all;
    Our good ship sails the morn.
Oh say not so, my master dear,
    For I fear a deadly storm.

Late, late yestreen I saw the new moon
    With the old moon in her arm,
And I fear, I fear, my master dear,
    That we will come to harm.

They hadna sailed a league, a league,
    A league but barely three,
When the air grew dark, and the wind blew loud,
    And growly grew the sea.

Oh our Scotch nobles were right loth
    To wet their cork-heeled shoon,
But long ere all the play were played
    Their hats they swam aboon.

Oh long, long may their ladies sit
    With their fans into their hand
Ere ever they see Sir Patrick Spens
    Come sailing to the land.

Oh long, long may the ladies stand
    With their gold combs in their hair
Waiting for their own dear lords,
    For they'll see them no more.

Half o'er, half o'er to Aberdour
    It's fifty fathom deep,
And there lies good Sir Patrick Spens
    With the Scotch lords at his feet.

17

ELDERS

I Go Back to May 1937

Sharon Olds

I see them standing at the formal gates of their colleges,
I see my father strolling out
under the ochre sandstone arch, the
red tiles glinting like bent
plates of blood behind his head, I
see my mother with a few light books at her hip
standing at the pillar made of tiny bricks with the
wrought-iron gate still open behind her, its
sword-tips black in the May air,
they are about to graduate, they are about to get married,
they are kids, they are dumb, all they know is they are
innocent, they would never hurt anybody.
I want to go up to them and say Stop,
don't do it—she's the wrong woman,
he's the wrong man, you are going to do things
you cannot imagine you would ever do,
you are going to do bad things to children,
you are going to suffer in ways you never heard of,
you are going to want to die. I want to go
up to them there in the late May sunlight and say it,
her hungry pretty blank face turning to me,
her pitiful beautiful untouched body,
his arrogant handsome blind face turning to me,
his pitiful beautiful untouched body,
but I don't do it. I want to live. I

take them up like the male and female
paper dolls and bang them together
at the hips like chips of flint as if to
strike sparks from them, I say
Do what you are going to do, and I will tell about it.

Those Winter Sundays

Robert Hayden

Sundays too my father got up early
and put his clothes on in the blueblack cold,
then with cracked hands that ached
from labor in the weekday weather made
banked fires blaze. No one ever thanked him.

I'd wake and hear the cold splintering, breaking.
When the rooms were warm, he'd call,
and slowly I would rise and dress,
fearing the chronic angers of that house,

Speaking indifferently to him,
who had driven out the cold
and polished my good shoes as well.
What did I know, what did I know
of love's austere and lonely offices?

The Old Liberators

Robert Hedin

Of all the people in the mornings at the mall,
It's the old liberators I like best,
Those veterans of the Bulge, Anzio, or Monte Cassino
I see lost in Automotive or back in Home Repair,
Bored among the paints and power tools.
Or the *really* old ones, the ones who are going fast,
Who keep dozing off in the little orchards
Of shade under the distant skylights.
All around, from one bright rack to another,
Their wives stride big as generals,
Their handbags bulging like ripe fruit.
They are almost all gone now,
And with them they are taking the flak
And fire storms, the names of the old bombing runs.
Each day a little more of their memory goes out,
Darkens the way a house darkens,
Its rooms quietly filling with evening,
Until nothing but the wind lifts the lace curtains,
The wind bearing through the empty rooms
The rich far off scent of gardens
Where just now, this morning,
Light is falling on the wild philodendrons.

To My Mother

Wendell Berry

I was your rebellious son,
do you remember? Sometimes
I wonder if you do remember,
so complete has your forgiveness been.

So complete has your forgiveness been
I wonder sometimes if it did not
precede my wrong, and I erred,
safe found, within your love,

prepared ahead of me, the way home,
or my bed at night, so that almost
I should forgive you, who perhaps
foresaw the worst that I might do,

and forgave before I could act,
causing me to smile now, looking back,
to see how paltry was my worst,
compared to your forgiveness of it

already given. And this, then,
is the vision of that Heaven of which
we have heard, where those who love
each other have forgiven each other,

where, for that, the leaves are green,
the light a music in the air,
and all is unentangled,
and all is undismayed.

Working in the Rain

Robert Morgan

My father loved more than anything to
work outside in wet weather. Beginning
at daylight he'd go out in dripping brush
to mow or pull weeds for hog and chickens.
First his shoulders got damp and the drops from
his hat ran down his back. When even his
armpits were soaked he came in to dry out
by the fire, make coffee, read a little.
But if the rain continued he'd soon be
restless, and go out to sharpen tools in
the shed or carry wood in from the pile,
then open up a puddle to the drain,
working by steps back into the downpour.
I thought he sought the privacy of rain,
the one time no one was likely to be
out and he was left to the intimacy
of drops touching every leaf and tree in
the woods and the easy muttering of
drip and runoff, the shine of pools behind
grass dams. He could not resist the long
ritual, the companionship and freedom
of falling weather, or even the cold
drenching, the heavy soak and chill of clothes
and sobbing of fingers and sacrifice
of shoes that earned a baking by the fire
and washed fatigue after the wandering
and loneliness in the country of rain.

Birthday Card to My Mother

Philip Appleman

The toughness indoor people have:
    the will
to brave confusion in
mohair sofas, crocheted doilies—challenging
in every tidy corner some
bit of the outdoor drift and sag;
    the tenacity
in forty quarts of cherries up for winter,
gallon churns of sherbet at
family reunions,
fifty thousand suppers cleared away;
    the tempering
of rent-men at the front door, hanging on,
light bills overdue,
sons off to war or buried, daughters
taking on the names of strangers.

You have come through
the years of wheelchairs, loneliness—
a generation of pain
knotting the joints like ancient apple trees;
you always knew
this was no world to be weak in:
where best friends wither to old
phone numbers in far-off towns;

where the sting of children is always
sharper than serpents' teeth; where
love itself goes shifting
and slipping away to shadows.

You have survived it all,
come through wreckage and triumph hard
at the center but spreading
gentleness around you—nowhere
by your bright hearth has the dust
of bitterness lain unswept;
today, thinking back, thinking ahead
to other birthdays, I
lean upon your courage
and sign this card, as always,
with love.

Yesterday

W. S. Merwin

My friend says I was not a good son
you understand
I say yes I understand

he says I did not go
to see my parents very often you know
and I say yes I know

even when I was living in the same city he says
maybe I would go there once
a month or maybe even less
I say oh yes

he says the last time I went to see my father
I say the last time I saw my father

he says the last time I saw my father
he was asking me about my life
how I was making out and he
went into the next room
to get something to give me

oh I say
feeling again the cold
of my father's hand the last time

he says and my father turned
in the doorway and saw me
look at my wristwatch and he
said you know I would like you to stay
and talk with me

oh yes I say

but if you are busy he said
I don't want you to feel that you
have to
just because I'm here

I say nothing

he says my father
said maybe
you have important work you are doing
or maybe you should be seeing
somebody I don't want to keep you

I look out the window
my friend is older than I am
he says and I told my father it was so
and I got up and left him then
you know

though there was nowhere I had to go
and nothing I had to do

No Map

Stephen Dobyns

How close the clouds press this October first
and the rain—a gray scarf across the sky.
In separate hospitals my father and a dear friend
lie waiting for their respective operations,
hours on a table as surgeons crack their chests.
They were so brave when I talked to them last
as they spoke of the good times we would share
in the future. To neither did I say how much
I loved them, nor express the extent of my fear.
Their bodies are delicate glass boxes
at which the world begins to fling its stones.
Is this the day their long cry will be released?
How can I live in this place without them?
But today is also my son's birthday.
He is eight and beginning his difficult march.
To him the sky is welcoming, the road straight.
Far from my house he will open his presents—
a book, a Swiss army knife, some music. Where
is his manual of instructions? Where is his map
showing the dark places and how to escape them?

My Mother

Robert Mezey

My mother writes from Trenton,
a comedian to the bone
but underneath serious
and all heart. 'Honey,' she says,
'be a mensch and Mary too,
its no good, to worry, you
are doing the best you can
your Dad and everyone
thinks you turned out very well
as long as you pay your bills
nobody can say a word
you can tell them, to drop dead
so save a dollar it can't
hurt—remember Frank you went
to highschool with? he still lives
with his wife's mother, his wife
works while he writes his books and
did he ever sell a one
the four kids run around naked
36, and he's never had,
you'll forgive my expression
even a pot to piss in
or a window to throw it,
such a smart boy he couldnt
read the footprints on the wall
honey you think you know all

the answers you dont, please, try
to put some money away
believe me it wouldn't hurt
artist shmartist life's too short
for that kind of, forgive me,
horseshit, I know what you want
better than you, all that counts
is to make a good living
and the best of everything,
as Sholem Aleichem said,
he was a great writer did
you ever read his books dear,
you should make what he makes a year
anyway he says some place
Poverty is no disgrace
but its no honor either
that's what I say,
    love,
     Mother'

When My Dead Father Called

Robert Bly

Last night I dreamt my father called to us.
He was stuck somewhere. It took us
A long time to dress, I don't know why.
The night was snowy; there were long black roads.

Finally, we reached the little town, Bellingham.
There he stood, by a streetlamp in cold wind,
Snow blowing along the sidewalk. I noticed
The uneven sort of shoes that men wore

In the early Forties. And overalls. He was smoking.
Why did it take us so long to get going? Perhaps
He left us somewhere once, or did I simply
Forget he was alone in winter in some town?

August Third

May Sarton

These days
Lifting myself up
Like a heavy weight,
Old camel getting to her knees,
I think of my mother
And the inexhaustible flame
That kept her alive
Until she died.

She knew all about fatigue
And how one pushes it aside
For staking up the lilies
Early in the morning,
The way one pushes it aside
For a friend in need,
For a hungry cat.

Mother, be with me.
Today on your birthday
I am older than you were
When you died
Thirty-five years ago.
Thinking of you
The old camel gets to her knees,
Stands up,

Moves forward slowly
Into the new day.

If you taught me one thing
It was never to fail life.

Terminus

Ralph Waldo Emerson

It is time to be old,
To take in sail:—
The god of bounds,
Who sets to seas a shore,
Come to me in his fatal rounds,
And said: 'No more!
No farther spread
Thy broad ambitious branches, and thy root.
Fancy departs: no more invent,
Contract thy firmament
To compass of a tent.
There's not enough for this and that,
Make thy option which of two;
Economize the failing river,
Not the less revere the Giver,
Leave the many and hold the few.
Timely wise accept the terms,
Soften the fall with wary foot;
A little while
Still plan and smile,
And—fault of novel germs—
Mature the unfallen fruit.

Curse, if thou wilt, thy sires,
Bad husbands of their fires,
Who, when they gave thee breath,

Failed to bequeath
The needful sinew stark as once,
The Baresark marrow to thy bones,
But left a legacy of ebbing veins,
Inconstant heat and nerveless reins,—
Amid the Muses, left thee deaf and dumb
Amid the gladiators, halt and numb.'

As the bird trims her to the gale,
I trim myself to the storm of time,
I man the rudder, reef the sail,
Obey the voice at eve obeyed at prime:
'Lowly faithful, banish fear,
Right onward drive unharmed;
The port, well worth the cruise, is near,
And every wave is charmed.'

18

THE END

Authorship

James B(all) Naylor

King David and King Solomon
　　　Led merry, merry lives,
With many, many lady friends
　　　And many, many wives;
But when old age crept over them,
　　　With many, many qualms,
King Solomon wrote the Proverbs
　　　And King David wrote the Psalms.

Young and Old

Charles Kingsley

When all the world is young, lad,
    And all the trees are green;
And every goose a swan, lad,
    And every lass a queen;
Then hey for boot and horse, lad,
    And round the world away;
Young blood must have its course, lad,
    And every dog his day.

When all the world is old, lad,
    And all the trees are brown;
And all the sport is stale, lad,
    And all the wheels run down;
Creep home, and take your place there,
    The spent and maimed among:
God grant you find one face there,
    You loved when all was young.

Shifting the Sun

Diana Der-Hovanessian

When your father dies, say the Irish,
you lose your umbrella against bad weather.
May his sun be your light, say the Armenians.

When your father dies, say the Welsh,
you sink a foot deeper into the earth.
May you inherit his light, say the Armenians.

When your father dies, say the Canadians,
you run out of excuses. May you inherit
his sun, say the Armenians.

When your father dies, say the French,
you become your own father.
May you stand up in his light, say the Armenians.

When your father dies, say the Indians,
he comes back as the thunder.
May you inherit his light, say the Armenians.

When your father dies, say the Russians,
he takes your childhood with him.
May you inherit his light, say the Armenians.

When your father dies, say the English,
you join his club you vowed you wouldn't.
May you inherit his sun, say the Armenians.

When your father dies, say the Armenians,
your sun shifts forever.
And you walk in his light.

My Dad's Wallet

Raymond Carver

Long before he thought of his own death,
my dad said he wanted to lie close
to his parents. He missed them so
after they went away.
He said this enough that my mother remembered,
and I remembered. But when the breath
left his lungs and all signs of life
had faded, he found himself in a town
512 miles away from where he wanted most to be.

My dad, though. He was restless
even in death. Even in death
he had this one last trip to take.
All his life he liked to wander,
and now he had one more place to get to.

The undertaker said he'd arrange it,
not to worry. Some poor light
from the window fell on the dusty floor
where we waited that afternoon
until the man came out of the back room
and peeled off his rubber gloves.
He carried the smell of formaldehyde with him.
He was a big man, this undertaker said.
Then began to tell us why
he liked living in this small town.

This man who'd just opened my dad's veins.
How much is it going to cost? I said.

He took out his pad and pen and began
to write. First, the preparation charges.
Then he figured the transportation
of the remains at 22 cents a mile.
But this was a round-trip for the undertaker,
don't forget. Plus, say, six meals
and two nights in a motel. He figured
some more. Add a surcharge of
$210 for his time and trouble,
and there you have it.

He thought we might argue.
There was a spot of color on
each of his cheeks as he looked up
from his figures. The same poor light
fell in the same poor place on
the dusty floor. My mother nodded
as if she understood. But she
hadn't understood a word of it.
None of it had made any sense to her,
beginning with the time she left home
with my dad. She only knew
that whatever was happening
was going to take money.
She reached into her purse and brought up
my dad's wallet. The three of us
in that little room that afternoon.
Our breath coming and going.

We stared at the wallet for a minute.
Nobody said anything.
All the life had gone out of that wallet.
It was old and rent and soiled.
But it was my dad's wallet. And she opened
it and looked inside. Drew out
a handful of money that would go
toward this last, most astounding, trip.

When I Am Asked

Lisel Mueller

When I am asked
how I began writing poems,
I talk about the indifference of nature.

It was soon after my mother died,
a brilliant June day,
everything blooming.

I sat on a gray stone bench
in a lovingly planted garden,
but the day lilies were as deaf
as the ears of drunken sleepers
and the roses curved inward.
Nothing was black or broken
and not a leaf fell
and the sun blared endless commercials
for summer holidays.

I sat on a gray stone bench
ringed with the ingenue faces
of pink and white impatiens
and placed my grief
in the mouth of language,
the only thing that would grieve with me.

Dirge Without Music

Edna St. Vincent Millay

I am not resigned to the shutting away of loving hearts in the
  hard ground.
So it is, and so it will be, for so it has been, time out of mind:
Into the darkness they go, the wise and the lovely. Crowned
With lilies and with laurel they go; but I am not resigned.

Lovers and thinkers, into the earth with you.
Be one with the dull, the indiscriminate dust.
A fragment of what you felt, of what you knew,
A formula, a phrase remains,—but the best is lost.

The answers quick and keen, the honest look, the laughter,
  the love,—
They are gone. They are gone to feed the roses. Elegant and
  curled
Is the blossom. Fragrant is the blossom. I know. But I do not
  approve.
More precious was the light in your eyes than all the roses in
  the world.

Down, down, down into the darkness of the grave
Gently they go, the beautiful, the tender, the kind;
Quietly they go, the intelligent, the witty, the brave.
I know. But I do not approve. And I am not resigned.

Donald Hall

My mother said, "Of course,
it may be nothing, but your father
    has a spot on his lung."
That was all that was said: My father
    at fifty-one could never
speak of dreadful things without tears.
    When I started home,
I kissed his cheek, which was not our habit.
    In a letter, my mother
asked me not to kiss him again
    because it made him sad.
In two weeks, the exploratory
    revealed an inoperable
lesion.
    The doctors never
    told him; he never asked,
but read *The Home Medical Guidebook.*
    Seven months later,
just after his fifty-second birthday
    —his eyesight going,
his voice reduced to a whisper, three days
    before he died—he said,
"If anything should happen to me . . ."

Departures

Linda Pastan

They seemed to all take off
at once: Aunt Grace
whose kidneys closed shop;
Cousin Rose who fed sugar
to diabetes;
my grandmother's friend
who postponed going so long
we thought she'd stay.

It was like the summer years ago
when they all set out on trains
and ships, wearing hats with veils
and the proper gloves,
because everybody was going
someplace that year,
and they didn't want
to be left behind.

As Befits a Man

Langston Hughes

I don't mind dying—
But I'd hate to die all alone!
I want a dozen pretty women
To holler, cry, and moan.

I don't mind dying
But I want my funeral to be fine:
A row of long tall mamas
Fainting, fanning, and crying.

I want a fish-tail hearse
And sixteen fish-tail cars,
A big brass band
And a whole truck load of flowers.

When they let me down,
Down into the clay,
I want the women to holler:
Please don't take him away!
        Ow-ooo-oo-o!
Don't take daddy away!

Sunt Leones

Stevie Smith

The lions who ate the Christians on the sands of the arena
By indulging native appetites played what has now been seen a
Not entirely negligible part
In consolidating at the very start
The position of the Early Christian Church.
Initiatory rites are always bloody
And the lions, it appears
From contemporary art, made a study
Of dyeing Coliseum sands a ruddy
Liturgically sacrificial hue
And if the Christians felt a little blue—
Well, people being eaten often do.
Theirs was the death, and theirs the crown undying,
A state of things which must be satisfying.
My point which up to this has been obscured
Is that it was the lions who procured
By chewing up blood gristle flesh and bone
The martyrdoms on which the Church has grown.
I only write this poem because I thought it rather looked
As if the part the lions played was being overlooked.
By lions' jaws great benefits and blessings were begotten
And so our debt to Lionhood must never be forgotten.

Perfection Wasted

John Updike

And another regrettable thing about death
is the ceasing of your own brand of magic,
which took a whole life to develop and market—
the quips, the witticisms, the slant
adjusted to a few, those loved ones nearest
the lip of the stage, their soft faces blanched
in the footlight glow, their laughter close to tears,
their tears confused with their diamond earrings,
their warm pooled breath in and out with your heartbeat,
their response and your performance twinned.
The jokes over the phone. The memories packed
in the rapid-access file. The whole act.
Who will do it again? That's it: no one;
imitators and descendants aren't the same.

Eleanor's Letters

Donald Hall

I who picked up the neat
Old letters never knew
The last names to complete
"Aunt Eleanor" or "Lew."

She talked about the weather,
And canning, and a trip
Which they might take together
"If we don't lose our grip."

But "Lew has got a growth
Which might turn out, they say,
Benign, or shrink, or both."
Then, "Lewis passed away."

He didn't *die.* That word
Seemed harsh and arbitrary
And thus was not preferred
In her vocabulary.

"Everything's for the better,"
She wrote, and what is more,
She signed her dying letter
"As ever, Eleanor."

Death and the Turtle

May Sarton

I watched the turtle dwindle day by day,
Get more remote, lie limp upon my hand;
When offered food he turned his head away;
The emerald shell grew soft. Quite near the end
Those withdrawn paws stretched out to grasp
His long head in a poignant dying gesture.
It was so strangely like a human clasp,
My heart cracked for the brother creature.

I buried him, wrapped in a lettuce leaf,
The vivid eye sunk inward, a dull stone.
So this was it, the universal grief:
Each bears his own end knit up in the bone.
Where are the dead? we ask, as we hurtle
Toward the dark, part of this strange creation,
One with each limpet, leaf, and smallest turtle—
Cry out for life, cry out in desperation!

Who will remember you when I have gone,
My darling ones, or who remember me?
Only in our wild hearts the dead live on.
Yet these frail engines bound to mystery
Break the harsh turn of all creation's wheel,
For we remember China, Greece, and Rome,
Our mothers and our fathers, and we steal
From death itself its rich store, and bring it home.

Four Poems in One

Anne Porter

At six o'clock this morning
I saw the rising sun
Resting on the ground like a boulder
In the thicket back of the school,
A single great ember
About the height of a man.

❖   ❖   ❖

Night has gone like a sickness,
The sky is pure and whole.
Our Lady of Poland spire
Is rosy with first light,
Starlings above it shatter their dark flock.
Notes of the Angelus
Leave their great iron cup
And slowly, three by three
Visit the Polish gardens round about,
Dahlias shaggy with frost
Sheds with their leaning tools
Rosebushes wrapped in burlap
Skiffs upside down on trestles
Like dishes after supper.

❖   ❖   ❖

These are the poems I'd show you
But you're no longer alive.
The cables creaked and shook
Lowering the heavy box.
The rented artificial grass
Still left exposed
That gritty gash of earth
Yellow and mixed with stones
Taking your body
That never in this world
Will we see again, or touch.

✧   ✧   ✧

We know little
We can tell less
But one thing I know
One thing I can tell
I will see you again in Jerusalem
Which is of such beauty
No matter what country you come from
You will be more at home there
Than ever with father or mother
Than even with lover or friend
And once we're within her borders
Death will hunt us in vain.

Titanic

David R. Slavitt

Who does not love the *Titanic*?
If they sold passage tomorrow for that same crossing,
who would not buy?

To go down . . . We all go down, mostly
alone. But with crowds of people, friends, servants,
well fed, with music, with lights! Ah!

And the world, shocked, mourns, as it ought to do
and almost never does. There will be the books and movies
to remind our grandchildren who we were
and how we died, and give them a good cry.

Not so bad, after all. The cold
water is anaesthetic and very quick.
The cries on all sides must be a comfort.

We all go: only a few, first class.

The Burial of Sir John Moore
after Corunna

Charles Wolfe

Not a drum was heard, not a funeral note,
　　As his corpse to the rampart we hurried;
Not a soldier discharged his farewell shot
　　O'er the grave where our hero we buried.

We buried him darkly at dead of night,
　　The sods with our bayonets turning,
By the struggling moonbeam's misty light
　　And the lanthorn dimly burning.

No useless coffin enclosed his breast,
　　Not in sheet or in shroud we wound him;
But he lay like a warrior taking his rest
　　With his martial cloak around him.

Few and short were the prayers we said,
　　And we spoke not a word of sorrow;
But we steadfastly gazed on the face that was dead,
　　And we bitterly thought of the morrow.

We thought, as we hollowed his narrow bed
　　And smoothed down his lonely pillow,
That the foe and the stranger would tread o'er his head,
　　And we far away on the billow!

Lightly they'll talk of the spirit that's gone,
    And o'er his cold ashes upbraid him —
But little he'll reck, if they let him sleep on
    In the grave where a Briton has laid him.

But half of our heavy task was done
    When the clock struck the hour for retiring;
And we heard the distant and random gun
    That the foe was sullenly firing.

Slowly and sadly we laid him down,
    From the field of his fame fresh and gory;
We carved not a line, and we raised not a stone,
    But we left him alone with his glory.

Kaddish

David Ignatow

Mother of my birth, for how long were we together
in your love and my adoration of your self?
For the shadow of a moment, as I breathed your pain
and you breathed my suffering. As we knew
of shadows in lit rooms that would swallow the light.

Your face beneath the oxygen tent was alive
but your eyes closed, your breathing hoarse.
Your sleep was with death. I was alone
with you as when I was young
but now only alone, not with you,
to become alone forever, as I was learning
watching you become alone.

Earth now is your mother, as you were mine, my earth,
my sustenance and my strength,
and now without you I turn to your mother
and seek from her that I may meet you again
in rock and stone. Whisper to the stone,
I love you. Whisper to the rock, I found you.
Whisper to the earth, Mother, I have found her,
and I am safe and always have been.

Twilight: After Haying

Jane Kenyon

Yes, long shadows go out
from the bales; and yes, the soul
must part from the body:
what else could it do?

The men sprawl near the baler,
too tired to leave the field.
They talk and smoke,
and the tips of their cigarettes
blaze like small roses
in the night air. (It arrived
and settled among them
before they were aware.)

The moon comes
to count the bales,
and the dispossessed—
Whip-poor-will, Whip-poor-will
—sings from the dusty stubble.

These things happen . . . the soul's bliss
and suffering are bound together
like the grasses . . .

The last, sweet exhalations
of timothy and vetch
go out with the song of the bird;
the ravaged field
grows wet with dew.

For the Anniversary of My Death

W. S. Merwin

Every year without knowing it I have passed the day
When the last fires will wave to me
And the silence will set out
Tireless traveler
Like the beam of a lightless star

Then I will no longer
Find myself in life as in a strange garment
Surprised at the earth
And the love of one woman
And then shamelessness of men
As today writing after three days of rain
Hearing the wren sing and the falling cease
And bowing not knowing to what

from The Old Italians Dying

Lawrence Ferlinghetti

For years the old Italians have been dying
all over America
For years the old Italians in faded felt hats
have been sunning themselves and dying
You have seen them on the benches
in the park in Washington Square
the old Italians in their black high button shoes
the old men in their old felt fedoras
                              with stained hatbands
have been dying and dying
                              day by day
You have seen them
every day in Washington Square San Francisco
the slow bell
tolls in the morning
in the Church of Peter & Paul
in the marzipan church on the plaza
toward ten in the morning the slow bell tolls
in the towers of Peter & Paul
and the old men who are still alive
sit sunning themselves in a row
on the wood benches in the park
and watch the processions in and out
funerals in the morning
weddings in the afternoon
slow bell in the morning Fast bell at noon

In one door out the other
the old men sit there in their hats
and watch the coming & going
You have seen them
the ones who feed the pigeons
                cutting the stale bread
                    with their thumbs & penknives
the ones with old pocketwatches
the old ones with gnarled hands
                    and wild eyebrows
the ones with the baggy pants
                    with both belt & suspenders
the grappa drinkers with teeth like corn
the Piemontesi the Genovesi the Sicilianos
                smelling of garlic & pepperonis
the ones who loved Mussolini
the old fascists
the ones who loved Garibaldi
the old anarchists reading *L'Umanita Nuova*
the ones who loved Sacco & Vanzetti
They are almost all gone now
They are sitting and waiting their turn
and sunning themselves in front of the church
over the doors of which is inscribed
a phrase which would seem to be unfinished
from Dante's *Paradiso*
about the glory of the One
                    who moves everything . . .
The old men are waiting
for it to be finished
for their glorious sentence on earth
                        to be finished

The End · 415

Street Ballad

George Barker

From high above the birds look down and sing because
    they see
the monstrous comedies they miss, living several storeys
    higher:
the dirty degradations and the gross humiliations,
they, like the gods, without pity, look down upon from a
    telephone wire.

But as they sit there high above and gaze down upon our
    brutal
short and messy circumstances, they do not see the one
who stands behind a cardboard tree examining them
    coldly
with one eye closed and the other staring along the barrel
    of a gun.

Let Evening Come

Jane Kenyon

Let the light of late afternoon
shine through chinks in the barn, moving
up the bales as the sun moves down.

Let the crickets take up chafing
as a woman takes up her needles
and her yarn. Let evening come.

Let dew collect on the hoe abandoned
in long grass. Let the stars appear
and the moon disclose her silver horn.

Let the fox go back to its sandy den.
Let the wind die down. Let the shed
go black inside. Let evening come.

To the bottle in the ditch, to the scoop
in the oats, to air in the lung
let evening come.

Let it come, as it will, and don't
be afraid. God does not leave us
comfortless, so let evening come.

19

THE RESURRECTION

Forty-Five

Hayden Carruth

When I was forty-five I lay for hours
beside a pool, the green hazy
springtime water, and watched
the salamanders coupling, how they drifted lazily,
their little hands floating before them,
aimlessly in and out of the shadows, fifteen
or twenty of them, and suddenly two
would dart together and clasp
one another belly to belly
the way we do, tender and vigorous, and then
would let go and drift away
at peace, lazily,
in the green pool that was their world
and for a while was mine.

A Blessing

James Wright

Just off the highway to Rochester, Minnesota,
Twilight bounds softly forth on the grass.
And the eyes of those two Indian ponies
Darken with kindness.
They have come gladly out of the willows
To welcome my friend and me.
We step over the barbed wire into the pasture
Where they have been grazing all day, alone.
They ripple tensely, they can hardly contain their happiness
That we have come.
They bow shyly as wet swans. They love each other.
There is no loneliness like theirs.
At home once more,
They begin munching the young tufts of spring in the
    darkness.
I would like to hold the slenderer one in my arms,
For she has walked over to me
And nuzzled my left hand.
She is black and white,
Her mane falls wild on her forehead,
And the light breeze moves me to caress her long ear
That is delicate as the skin over a girl's wrist.
Suddenly I realize
That if I stepped out of my body I would break
Into blossom.

Holy Thursday

William Blake

'Twas on a Holy Thursday, their innocent faces clean,
The children walking two & two, in red & blue & green,
Grey-headed beadles walked before with wands as white as snow,
Till into the high dome of Paul's they like Thames' waters flow.

O what a multitude they seemed, these flowers of London town!
Seated in companies they sit with radiance all their own.
The hum of multitudes was there, but multitudes of lambs,
Thousands of little boys & girls raising their innocent hands.

Now like a mighty wind they raise to Heaven the voice of song,
Or like harmonious thunderings the seats of Heaven among.
Beneath them sit the aged men, wise guardians of the poor;
Then cherish pity, lest you drive an angel from your door.

from Walden

Henry David Thoreau

The life in us is like the water in the river. It may rise this year higher than man has ever known it, and flood the parched uplands; even this may be the eventful year, which will drown out all our muskrats. It was not always dry land where we dwell. I see far inland the banks which the stream anciently washed, before science began to record its freshets. Every one has heard the story which has gone the rounds of New England, of a strong and beautiful bug which came out of the dry leaf of an old table of apple-tree wood, which had stood in a farmer's kitchen for sixty years, first in Connecticut, and afterward in Massachusetts,—from an egg deposited in the living tree many years earlier still, as appeared by counting the annual layers beyond it; which was heard gnawing out for several weeks, hatched perchance by the heat of an urn. Who does not feel his faith in a resurrection and immortality strengthened by hearing of this? Who knows what beautiful and winged life, whose egg has been buried for ages under many concentric layers of woodenness in the dead dry life of society, deposited at first in the alburnum of the green and living tree, which has been gradually converted into the semblance of its well-seasoned tomb,—heard perchance gnawing out now for years by the astonished family of man, as they sat round the festive board,—may unexpectedly come forth from amidst society's most trivial and handselled furniture, to enjoy its perfect summer life at last!

I do not say that John or Jonathan will realize all this; but such is the character of that morrow which mere lapse of time can never

make to dawn. The light which puts out our eyes is darkness to us.
Only that day dawns to which we are awake. There is more
day to dawn. The sun is but a morning star.

The Peace of Wild Things

Wendell Berry

When despair for the world grows in me
and I wake in the night at the least sound
in fear of what my life and my children's lives may be,
I go and lie down where the wood drake
rests in his beauty on the water, and the great heron feeds.
I come into the peace of wild things
who do not tax their lives with forethought
of grief. I come into the presence of still water.
And I feel above me the day-blind stars
waiting with their light. For a time
I rest in the grace of the world, and am free.

From Blossoms

Li-Young Lee

From blossoms comes
this brown paper bag of peaches
we bought from the boy
at the bend in the road where we turned toward
signs painted Peaches.

From laden boughs, from hands,
from sweet fellowship in the bins,
comes nectar at the roadside, succulent
peaches we devour, dusty skin and all,
comes the familiar dust of summer, dust we eat.

O, to take what we love inside,
to carry within us an orchard, to eat
not only the skin, but the shade,
not only the sugar, but the days, to hold
the fruit in our hands, adore it, then bite into
the round jubilance of peach.

There are days we live
as if death were nowhere
in the background; from joy
to joy to joy, from wing to wing,
from blossom to blossom to
impossible blossom, to sweet impossible blossom.

The First Green of Spring

David Budbill

Out walking in the swamp picking cowslip, marsh marigold,
this sweet first green of spring. Now sautéed in a pan melting
to a deeper green than ever they were alive, this green, this life,

harbinger of things to come. Now we sit at the table munching
on this message from the dawn which says we and the world
are alive again today, and this is the world's birthday. And

even though we know we are growing old, we are dying, we
will never be young again, we also know we're still right here
now, today, and, my oh my! don't these greens taste good.

Here

Grace Paley

Here I am in the garden laughing
an old woman with heavy breasts
and a nicely mapped face

how did this happen
well that's who I wanted to be

at last   a woman
in the old style   sitting
stout thighs apart under
a big skirt   grandchild sliding
on   off my lap   a pleasant
summer perspiration

that's my old man across the yard
he's talking to the meter reader
he's telling him the world's sad story
how electricity is oil or uranium
and so forth   I tell my grandson
run over to your grandpa   ask him
to sit beside me for a minute   I
am suddenly exhausted by my desire
to kiss his sweet explaining lips

The Lives of the Heart

Jane Hirshfield

Are ligneous, muscular, chemical.
Wear birch-colored feathers,
green tunnels of horse-tail reed.
Wear calcified spirals, Fibonaccian spheres.
Are edible; are glassy; are clay; blue schist.
Can be burned as tallow, as coal,
can be skinned for garnets, for shoes.
Cast shadows or light;
shuffle; snort; cry out in passion.
Are salt, are bitter,
tear sweet grass with their teeth.
Step silently into blue needle-fall at dawn.
Thrash in the net until hit.
Rise up as cities, as serpentined magma, as maples,
hiss lava-red into the sea.
Leave the strange kiss of their bodies
in Burgess Shale. Can be found, can be lost,
can be carried, broken, sung.
Lie dormant until they are opened by ice,
by drought. Go blind in the service of lace.
Are starving, are sated, indifferent, curious, mad.
Are stamped out in plastic, in tin.
Are stubborn, are careful, are slipshod,
are strung on the blue backs of flies
on the black backs of cows.
Wander the vacant whale-roads, the white thickets

heavy with slaughter.
Wander the fragrant carpets of alpine flowers.
Not one is not held in the arms of the rest, to blossom.
Not one is not given to ecstasy's lions.
Not one does not grieve.
Each of them opens and closes, closes and opens
the heavy gate—violent, serene, consenting, suffering it all.

Spring

Gerard Manley Hopkins

Nothing is so beautiful as spring—
    When weeds, in wheels, shoot long and lovely and lush;
    Thrush's eggs look little low heavens, and thrush
Through the echoing timber does so rinse and wring
The ear, it strikes like lightnings to hear him sing;
    The glassy peartree leaves and blooms, they brush
    The descending blue; that blue is all in a rush
With richness; the racing lambs too have fair their fling.

What is all this juice and all this joy?
    A strain of the earth's sweet being in the beginning
In Eden garden.—Have, get, before it cloy,
    Before it cloud, Christ, lord, and sour with sinning,
Innocent mind and Mayday in girl and boy,
    Most, O maid's child, thy choice and worthy the winning.

Fishing in the Keep of Silence

Linda Gregg

There is a hush now while the hills rise up
and God is going to sleep. He trusts the ship
of Heaven to take over and proceed beautifully
as he lies dreaming in the lap of the world.
He knows the owls will guard the sweetness
of the soul in their massive keep of silence,
looking out with eyes open or closed over
the length of Tomales Bay that the herons
conform to, whitely broad in flight, white
and slim in standing. God, who thinks about
poetry all the time, breathes happily as He
repeats to Himself: There are fish in the net,
lots of fish this time in the net of the heart.

Biographies

Ginger ANDREWS (1956, North Bend, OR) lives there still, teaching Sunday School at the Church of Christ, cleaning houses for a living. Her first book was *An Honest Answer.*

Philip APPLEMAN (1926, Kendallville, IN) served in the Army Air Corps in World War II. He taught English for many years at Indiana University and wrote books—three novels (including *Apes and Angels*), nonfiction (including the *Norton Critical Edition, Darwin*), and at least seven volumes of poetry.

Bob ARNOLD (1952, Adams, MA) is a carpenter and stonemason and poet whose family owns the oldest family lumber business in America, Arnold Lumber. *I took off for the woods after high school and don't plan ever to come out.*

W. H. AUDEN (1907–1973) left England for America in 1939, leaving behind his belief in socialism and Freud and finding a new life as a believing Anglican. His best known work, the poems found in most anthologies, "September 1, 1939" and "As I Walked Out One Evening" and "In Memory of W. B. Yeats" and "To An Unknown Citizen," all appeared in *Another Time* (1940), but the good man marched on, as essayist, editor, librettist (*The Rake's Progress*), playwright, poet, and teacher (his students called him Uncle Wiz). He wrote about his conversion to Anglicanism in *The Sea and the Mirror.* There is now a W. H. Auden Society in London. *Art is born of humiliation . . . Comedy is the noblest form of Stoicism. Among those whom I like or admire, I can find no common denominator, but among those whom I love, I can: all of them make me laugh.*

George BARKER (1913, Essex, England) was a friend of Dylan Thomas, a protégé of T. S. Eliot, and renowned for his romantic life: he fathered fifteen children in several different countries, including three in one summer.

Kate BARNES (1932, Maine) lives on a farm near Appleton, Maine, where she raises hay and blueberries. Her work is in *Crossing the Field* and *Where the Deer Were*.

Hilaire BELLOC (1870–1953) was the son of a French lawyer and an English suffragist, known now mainly for his light verse, though a prolific writer of astonishingly broad range: history, criticism, social and religious commentary, travel essays, journalism of all sorts—someone called him "the man who wrote a library." His work fell into disfavor in large part because his conservative Catholic views were unfashionable.

Wendell BERRY (1934, Newcastle, KY) is poet, essayist, novelist, farmer (near Port Royal, KY), environmentalist. *Breathe with unconditioned breath the unconditioned air. Shun electric wire. Communicate slowly. Live a three-dimensioned life; stay away from screens.*

John BERRYMAN (1914–1972) was an impassioned scholar, critic, and teacher in addition to poet, and the author of important studies of Shakespeare, Thomas Nashe, and Stephen Crane. His first big poem was *Homage to Mistress Bradstreet* in 1956, and then there were *The Dream Songs*, 385 of them, in 1969. Despite a chaotic life, in and out of hospitals, troubled by alcoholism, depression, and romantic turmoil, he was an impassioned and steadfast teacher and writer to the end of his days, a suicide.

Elizabeth BISHOP (1911–1979) wrote precisely and brilliantly about the physical world in her small body of work, *The Complete Poems* (1969). She drew from her childhood in Nova Scotia—where she was raised by grandparents—her travels in Europe, her time in Key West and New York, and sixteen years in Brazil.

William BLAKE (1757–1827) was an engraver and mystic and artist who illustrated his own poems, "Songs of Innocence" (1789) and "Songs of Experience" (1794).

Roy BLOUNT, Jr. (1941, Indianapolis, IN) grew up in Decatur, GA, and went to Vanderbilt. He is a lecturer on gender and aging, a screenwriter and dramatist, the author of *About Three Bricks Shy of a Load, Crackers, Be Sweet*, and editor of *Roy Blount's Book of Southern Humor*.

Robert BLY (1926, Madison, MN) was the son of Norwegian farmers ("I tried to become a playwright . . . the trouble was that nobody in my family talked") who, after the navy and Harvard, spent three years living down and out in New York, working odd jobs, sleeping in Grand Central when necessary, writing incessantly. Determined to stay clear of universities, having discovered the work of Pablo Neruda, Cesar Vallejo, Georg Trakl, and other major poets little known in literary academia, he moved back to Minnesota in 1955, to a farm near his parents', where he set out to promote foreign poets (and to insult the great sacred elephants of American lit) in his magazine *The Fifties*, which became *The Sixties* and then *The Seventies*. His *Silence in the Snowy Fields* came out in 1962. A wildly prolific writer and translator and editor and performer at workshops, he burst into best-sellerdom in 1990 with *Iron John: A Book About Men*, a treatise on the Grimm Brothers fairy tale. His most recent work is in *Morning Poems* and *The Night Abraham Called to the Stars*. *Donald Hall and I have been sending poems back and forth twice a week for forty years. At one time, we had a 48-hour rule: the other had to answer within 48 hours. My generation did a lot with letters. Galway Kinnell and Louis Simpson and Don and I and James Wright would often send five- and six-page typed letters commenting on and arguing with each others' poems. I'm amazed we had the time for that. Tranströmer and I exchanged hundreds of letters. The gist of it is that no one writes alone: One needs a community.*

Lucille BOGAN (1897–1948) was born in Amory, Mississippi, and made her first blues recordings in 1923, in New York, for the Okeh label. She took the name "Bessie Jackson" briefly in the thirties. Her risqué lyrics in songs such as "Shave 'Em Dry," "Women Won't Need No Men," and "Tricks Ain't Walkin' No More" were surely one reason her career was short and bumpy.

Philip BOOTH (1925, Hanover, NH) lives on the coast of Maine, in a house he lived in as a boy. His first book was *Letters from a Distant Land* (1957).

Sharon BRYAN (1951, Port Townsend, WA) studied philosophy and linguistics. *Benjamin Whorf's sense of the primacy of language meshes with my own . . . that language determines what we see, that a given language shapes its user's reality.*

David BUDBILL (1940, Cleveland) is the son of a streetcar motorman and lives in the mountains of northern Vermont. His play *Judevine*, about a poet on a mountain in Vermont, asks: *What good is my humility when I am stuck in this obscurity?* has been widely produced.

Charles BUKOWSKI (1920–1994) grew up poor in Los Angeles. He was a scrapper—abused by his father, scarred by acne, and given to drink—who struggled to get published. He earned his living at dozens of jobs including truck driver, dishwasher, and parking lot attendant; you get some idea of his style and directness from the titles of his books: *Flower, Fist and Bestial Wail; Longshot Pomes for Broke Players; All the Assholes in the World and Mine; To Kiss the Worms Goodnight; Love Is a Dog from Hell; Septuagenarian Stew.* Black Sparrow Press was founded by his friend John Martin to publish Bukowski's work.

Robert BURNS (1759–1796) is the national poet of Scotland, born to a family of tenant farmers, a champion of the poor and downtrodden, an enemy of Scottish Calvinism.

Hayden CARRUTH (1921, Waterbury, CT) one associates with rural Vermont and upstate New York, with politics, with jazz and the blues. A prolific poet, with at least twenty-nine books to his credit, including *Collected Longer Poems, Collected Shorter Poems,* and *Scrambled Eggs and Whiskey,* and also his long poem, *The Sleeping Beauty.*

Charles E. CARRYL (1841–1920) was a successful New York securities man with a seat on the stock exchange for thirty-four years who had a parallel career as a writer of nonsense and fantasy for children. *Davy and The Goblin* (1885) is a story of a little boy on a "believing voyage" that begins on a snowy Christmas Eve, the boy reading Lewis Carroll.

Raymond CARVER (1938–1988) came from Clatskanie, Oregon, grew up in Yakima, and wound up his short life in Port Angeles, Washington, where he is buried in a grave overlooking the Strait of Juan de Fuca. He came from difficult, hard-working, hard-drinking people, and once described himself as *a cigarette with a body attached to it* who went in for *full-time drinking as a serious pursuit,* though he found his way to diligent sobriety. His realistic Chekhovian prose fiction is well-known: *Will You Please Be Quiet, Please?, Cathedral,* and *What We Talk About When We Talk About Love.*

John CLARE (1793–1864) was the son of a farm worker in Northhamptonshire, largely self-taught, whose *Poems Descriptive of Rural Life* (1820) was well received but whose ill treatment at the hands of editors led to his mental breakdown. He spent his last two decades in an insane asylum.

Thomas CLARK (1944, Greenock, Scotland) grew up on the river Clyde, west of Glasgow, and now lives in Gloucestershire, England, though his poetry is still largely set in the Highlands and Western Islands. He and his wife, the artist Laurie Clark, direct the Cairn Gallery in the town of Nailsworth.

Billy COLLINS (1941, New York City) came to prominence in the nineties with a string of collections (*Picnic, Lightning; Questions About Angels;* and *The Art of Drowning*) of witty, well-crafted, good-hearted poems. *By the end of a poem, the reader should be in a different place from where he started. I would like him to be slightly disoriented at the end, like I drove him outside of town at night and dropped him off in a cornfield.*

Wendy COPE (1945, Kent, England) burst into view in 1986 with a collection of parodies and poems, *Making Cocoa for Kingsley Amis,* a best-seller in England. *I dislike the term "light verse" because it is used as a way of dismissing poets who allow humor into their work. I believe that a humorous poem can also be "serious," deeply felt, and say something that matters.*

Jimmie COX was a black composer of the twenties, about whom nothing is found in the standard reference works, but his song of 1923, "Nobody Knows You When You're Down and Out," was recorded by Bessie Smith.

E. E. CUMMINGS (1894–1962) lived in Patchin Place in Greenwich Village and died while chopping wood at his farm in New Hampshire in the fall. He had the good fortune, while an ambulance driver in France during World War I, to be detained by the authorities for six months, which gave him his first book, *The Enormous Room.* His unorthodox typography, especially the childish affectation of lowercase letters, has been imitated widely by lesser talents. His *95 Poems* is a classic. *I can express (my theory of technique) in fifteen words, by quoting The Eternal Question And Immortal Answer of burlesque, viz. "Would you hit a woman with a baby?—No, I'd hit her with a brick." Like the burlesque comedian, I am abnormally fond of that precision which creates movement.*

Leo DANGEL, a native of South Dakota, is author of *Old Man Brunner Country,* poems later adapted for the stage, and *Home from the Field.*

Roy DANIELLS (1902–1979) was a Canadian poet and scholar at universities in Manitoba and British Columbia.

W. H. DAVIES (1871–1940) was a Welsh poet and writer who worked his way around Europe as a cattle wrangler and fruit picker, and wrote about it in *Autobiography of a Supertramp* (1908), which came out with a preface by G. B. Shaw and made Davies famous and launched him on a career as novelist and poet.

Diana DER-HOVANNESSIAN (Worcester, MA). *My Armenian ancestry speaks in a lot of what I say. Armenia is a perfect laboratory for anyone to study the history of poetry. Here in one place is a long unbroken chain of the art, from pagan days through the time of Christian hymns, from simple folk poems to the time of Turkish oppressions, when poetry with oblique messages had to provide the sense of history and pride to keep a people intact.*

Emily DICKINSON (1830–1886) lived quietly in her father's house in Amherst, MA, and spent the last twenty-five years of her life a virtual recluse, while composing more than a thousand brief lyrics, some revised, others jotted down on scraps of paper. Only six were published in her lifetime, none with her consent. A few she showed to select friends, most she kept secret even from her family. From the mass of slips of paper she left behind, various collections were published, from 1890 on, edited by feuding heirs and executors, until Thomas H. Johnson's three-volume *The Poems of Emily Dickinson* came out in 1955. *The Manuscript Books of Emily Dickinson* (1982) reproduces 1,147 poems in facsimile. *If I read a book and it makes my whole body so cold no fire can ever warm me, I know that is poetry. If I feel physically as if the top of my head were taken off, I know that is poetry.*

Thomas M. DISCH (1940, Des Moines) is a busy and prolific author of science fiction (*Camp Concentration, 334, The MD*), criticism (*The Castle of Indolence,* an attack on the poetry "establishment," and *The Dreams Our Stuff is Made Of: How Science Fiction Conquered the World*), and poetry (*A Child's Garden of Grammar*).

Stuart DISCHELL (1954, Atlantic City) teaches at North Carolina. Among his books are *Good Hope Road* and *Evenings & Avenues.*

Stephen DOBYNS (1941, Orange, NJ) began as a police reporter for the Detroit *News*. In addition to his poetry (*Cemetery Nights, Body Traffic, Velocities*), he's written novels, including a popular series of detective books, the Bradshaw mysteries.

Keith DOUGLAS (1920–1944) served in North Africa in a British tank battalion and was killed in the D-Day invasion at Normandy.

Stephen DUNN (1939, New York) played on Hofstra University's championship team (25–1) of 1962, served in the army, considered a job as a newspaper reporter, and decided he felt queasy about asking questions of strangers. Instead he went to work writing brochures for Nabisco, was good at it, quit, went to Spain with his wife, and started writing seriously. He won the Pulitzer Prize for *Different Hours*. He lives in southern New Jersey. *My mother may have contributed to my ability to keep going in the face of uncertainty and neglect. She loved me unconditionally, and I've learned that such love breeds a kind of confidence, however wrong-headed, that things will turn out all right for you.*

R. W. EMERSON (1803–1882) was unhappy as a Boston clergyman and lasted only three years in the pulpit ("I like the silent church before the service begins, better than any preaching") whereupon he sailed to Europe for inspiration and returned to become a man of letters, writing, lecturing, shaking the gates of orthodoxy, befriending other writers, and gradually, like so many American dissenters, becoming a Grand Old Man and something of an institution. *You shall have joy, or you shall have power, said God; you shall not have both.*

Gavin EWART (1916–1995) was a virtuoso comic poet of England, author of *The Young Pobble's Guide to His Toes* and *The Gavin Ewart Show: Selected Poems 1939–1985*, the bard of army and corporate and family life, and sex. He was an ad writer for many years and edited the *Penguin Book of Light Verse*. *Miss Twye was soaping her breasts in her bath/When she heard behind her a meaningful laugh/And to her amazement she discovered/A wicked man in the bathroom cupboard.*

B. H. FAIRCHILD (Houston) grew up in small towns in west Texas, Oklahoma, and Kansas. He lives in Claremont, CA, and won the $100,000 Kingsley Tufts Poetry Award in 1999.

Lawrence FERLINGHETTI (1919, Yonkers, NY) is the proprietor of City Lights (at Broadway & Columbus in the North Beach section of San Francisco), a literary landmark since the fifties, a bookstore, and publisher of the Pocket Poets series of which Allen Ginsberg's "Howl" was No. 4. He fought in World War II and was sent to Nagasaki six weeks after its destruction. On the G.I. Bill, he studied art in Paris at the Sorbonne. *What it takes for great poetry is hunger and passion.*

Edward FIELD (1924, Brooklyn) is a former child cellist who flew twenty-five missions over Europe in World War II, after which he remained in Europe for two years and began to write.

Robert FROST (1847–1963) was farmer, schoolteacher, shoemaker, and finally poet, who, from the publication of *North of Boston* in 1914, was widely read and admired, a public career of almost fifty years. Shrewdly, he adopted a genial public persona of the homely Yankee farmer, behind which lived a troubled and restless man and a consummate lyrical poet. To the Frost persona was given a stream of honors and awards, and thus the poet was sustained. *It is only a moment here and a moment there that the greatest writer has. . . . Poetry is a way of taking life by the throat.*

Tess GALLAGHER (1943, Port Angeles, WA) lives in Port Angeles, looking out at the Puget Sound.

Deborah GARRISON (1965, Ann Arbor) works in an office in midtown Manhattan and writes poetry at night.

Dana GIOIA (1950, Los Angeles) studied with Elizabeth Bishop and Robert Fitzgerald at Harvard, then went into business for fifteen years, becoming a vice president at General Foods, upon which he quit to be able to write full-time. His 1991 essay, "Can Poetry Matter?," said that poetry had become *the specialized occupation of a relatively small and isolated group,* which sparked a fine controversy—especially the word "isolated." A formalist who argues for the power of storytelling in poetry, Gioia has written long narrative poems such as "The Homecoming."

Linda GREGG (1942, Suffern, NY) grew up in Marin County, CA, and lives there and in Northampton, MA. Her books include *Chosen by the Lion, Alma,* and *Too Bright to See.*

Arthur GUITERMAN (1871–1943) wrote many books of humorous verse, from *Betel Nuts, What They Say In Hindustan* (1907) to *Brave Laughter* (1943). *The Puritans fell upon their knees and then upon the aborigines.*

Donald HALL (1928, New Haven) has written since childhood. He went to Harvard with John Ashbery, Robert Bly, Frank O'Hara, Kenneth Koch, and Adrienne Rich. He taught for almost twenty years at the University of Michigan, then returned to his ancestral farm in New Hampshire to make his way as a freelance writer of criticism, memoirs, sports journalism, children's books, reviews, and more than fourteen books of poetry (and twenty-two of prose).

C. G. HANZLICEK (1942, Owatonna, MN) taught for more than thirty years at California State University at Fresno.

Robert HASS (1941, San Francisco) teaches at Berkeley. He has translated several books of poems by his friend Czeslaw Milosz.

Robert HAYDEN (1913–1980) grew up black and poor in Detroit, was befriended by local librarians and scholarshipped to Wayne State, then the University of Michigan. He taught at Fisk for many years, then Michigan, and in 1966 came under severe criticism from other black writers and critics for his lack of militance (he was Baha'I). He was the first black poet to be named consultant in poetry to the Library of Congress, a post later renamed Poet Laureate.

Seamus HEANEY (1939, County Derry, Northern Ireland) is the son of a farmer and the oldest of nine children. A schoolteacher, he left the North in 1972 to settle near Dublin and devote himself to writing, but with teaching stints in Ireland and also at Harvard. The Nobel Prize for Literature came his way in 1995. *The really valuable thing about my childhood was the verity of the life I lived within the house and the sense of trust that I had among the people on the ground . . . I like to feel that the line I am writing is being paid out from some old inner voice-reel, that it is coming up from the place I re-enter every time I go back to where I grew up. I still live a kind of den life when I go home, among my brothers and sisters in County Derry.*

Jennifer Michael HECHT (1965, Long Island) lives in the East Village in New York City. *The two poems here come from how difficult it is to keep trying year after year and how sweetly human, obvious, and yet remarkable it is to finally, on some given day, set down one's instruments of labor or remembering or mourning and walk away.*

Robert HEDIN (1949, Red Wing, MN) lived in Alaska and North Carolina, then migrated back to the Mississippi River valley.

J. F. HENDRY (1912, Glasgow) was a major in the British Army and a scholar and teacher of many languages.

Tom HENNEN (1942, Morris, MN) is a former park ranger and poet.

Geof HEWITT (1943, Glen Ridge, NJ) is a Vermonter who decided to be a writer after seeing Burt Lancaster in the movie *Youngblood Hawke.*

Jane HIRSHFIELD grew up in Manhattan, went to Princeton ('73), worked on a farm for a year, studied Zen Buddhism full time for eight years, and became a freelance editor. (Thomas Moore's *The Care of the Soul* was one of her projects.) She is the author of many books of poems, including *Three Foxes by the Edge of the Field at Twilight*, *The Love of Aged Horses*, *The Lives of the Heart*, and a book of essays, *Nine Gates: Entering the Mind of Poetry*. She lives in Mill Valley, CA. *Lyric poetry records our fidelity to the life of this earth even as we know that it will inevitably be lost.*

Bill HOLM (1943, Minneota, MN) lives in Minnesota (*a very small dot on an ocean of grass*) and in Iceland and travels to odd and interesting places—New Mexico, Madagascar, China—which he has written about in *Coming Home Crazy* and *Eccentric Islands*.

Gerard Manley HOPKINS (1844–1889) was born to a wealthy and artistic Stratford family and went off to Balliol College at Oxford where he converted to Catholicism, decided to become a priest, burned all his poems, and left for a Jesuit novitiate. Moved by the deaths of five nuns aboard a ship that sank in 1875, the *Deutschland*, he began writing poems again and continued (in his bucketa-bucketa style, what he called "sprung rhythm," which he got from reading Welsh poetry) through his years as parish priest in the slums of Manchester, Liverpool, and Glasgow, and during his time in Dublin teaching Greek at Royal University College, until his death, of typhoid, at the age of forty-five. His poems were not published until his friend Robert Bridges edited a volume of them in 1918.

Erica-Lynn HUBERTY (Gambino) (1969, New York City) is a poet and also a fine artist.

David HUDDLE (1942, Ivanhoe, VA) was a parachutist in Vietnam. He lives in Vermont, where he writes fiction and essays as well as poetry. *On those occasions when one's serenity seems about to collapse, I recommend that one step out into the backyard and vigorously spit.*

Langston HUGHES (1902–1967) grew up in Missouri, then Illinois, then, after a year at Columbia, traveled widely to Africa and Europe, before settling in Harlem in 1924. His *Weary Blues* came out in 1926. *I visited Paris, Milan, Venice, Geneva. I suffered a lot. I worked in the humblest places. I got to know the pains of the town up close. I went to Dakar, Nigeria, Luanda. The contact with those sweet people who had had their arms cut off by Belgians and their forests brutally laid to waste by France helped me understand that it was necessary to be these people's friend, their voice, their comfort, to be their poet. I have no other ambition than to be the poet of the blacks.*

David IGNATOW (1914–1997) was a New Yorker born in Brooklyn, and a teacher at NYU, Columbia, the New School, and Vassar. His *New and Collected Poems* came out in 1986.

Mark IRWIN (1953, Faribault, MN) has lived in France, Italy, Romania, and now in Denver. His work is in *Quick, Now, Always* and *White City* and other books.

Randall JARRELL (1914–1965) was a control tower operator for the Army in World War II and came to wide attention with *Little Friend, Little Friend* in 1945, based on his soldiering experience.

Louis JENKINS (1942, Oklahoma City) writes poems in his head walking around Duluth, Minnesota. *To write poetry is to try to say the unsayable. If it isn't beyond you, then it isn't worth doing. . . . It is a desperate act.*

Richard JONES (1953, London), son of a U.S. Air Force officer, lives in Chicago and writes poems (*Country of Air, At Last We Enter Paradise,* and *A Perfect Time*) and edits *Poetry East,* which he founded.

Erica JONG (1942, New York City) left Columbia midway through her Ph.D. program in eighteenth-century lit to write a novel, a big best seller in 1973, *Fear of Flying,* a depiction of "a thinking woman who also had a sexual life." *Any smart woman knows that the world is designed for the benefit of men, no matter how men whine about it. The trouble with The Women's Revolution is that we have not gone far enough because we indulge our fathers, husbands, brothers, sons. Also we feel sorry for them because they are led around by their dicks and their brains go soft. We accept the burden of being rational cause we know they're testosterone-driven.*

Donald JUSTICE (1925, Miami) grew up in Miami in the Depression, an only child of hard-working southern Baptists, was dazzled by Dostoevsky and poetry, and moved north to study with Berryman, Robert Lowell, and Karl Shapiro. He taught many places, including the University of Florida, and then retired, weary of debating the deconstructionists, *people who'd read Foucault but never looked at Tolstoy.* He disliked their *jargon and their grammar, their vast intellectual pretensions, their easy disdain for things they knew little or nothing about and had no interest in, their lousy taste in literature and the other arts, their nasty politicking, their hatred of the past and the tradition in favor of the fashionable and the perfectly silly.*

Julia KASDORF (1962, Lewistown, PA) grew up Mennonite and told stories about her people in *Sleeping Preacher* (1992). *It's not a culture of individual reflection or individual identity. It's not useful to sit around and think about yourself in that world. It's a world of collective identity, and storytelling is a form of collective writing.*

X. J. KENNEDY (1929, Dover. NJ) has written verse and fiction for children, and he and his wife Dorothy edited *Knock at a Star: A Child's Introduction to Poetry.* His first book was *Nude Descending a Staircase* in 1961.

Jane KENYON (1947–1995) grew up in Ann Arbor, where she studied at the University of Michigan. In 1972, she married her teacher, Donald Hall, and moved with him to Eagle Pond, New Hampshire, where she spent the rest of her life.

T. S. KERRIGAN (1939, Los Angeles) is a playwright and poet and a member of the Los Angeles Drama Critics Circle, and author of *Branches Among the Stars*, a two-act play about the young James Joyce in Dublin.

Charles KINGSLEY (1819–1875) was a curate, a Christian socialist, a professor of history, and a novelist, author of *Alton Locke* (1850) about the plight of farm workers, and his famous *The Water Babies* (1863), about a young chimney sweep who tries to escape his brutal life, falls into a river, and is transformed into a water baby.

Galway KINNELL (1927, Providence, RI) served in the navy, went to Paris on a Fulbright, worked in voter registration in the South, traveled widely in the Middle East and Europe, taught here and there. His first book was *What a Kingdom It Was* (1960), followed by *Flower Herding on Mount Monadnock, Body Rags, The Avenue Bearing the Initial of Christ into the New World: Poems 1946–1964*, and others. *There's not a specific something I'm aiming for, but there is something that's almost unspeakable and poems are efforts to speak it bit by bit, like a burden that has to be laid down piece by piece, that can't be thrown off.*

Maxine KUMIN (1925, Philadelphia) is a prolific writer of novels, short stories, more than twenty children's books, four books of essays, memoirs (*Inside the Halo* and *Beyond: The Anatomy of a Recovery*), and eleven books of poetry. And crime fiction. She lives on a farm in New Hampshire. *I feel great compassion and sorrow for people who have to live in high-rises. It would be the death of me. If I couldn't open the door and put my feet on earth, I think I would languish and just fade away.*

Stanley KUNITZ (1905, Worcester, MA) went to Harvard, then to New York to become an editor. His first book of poems, *Intellectual Things*, came out to scant notice in 1930, and he waited fourteen years to bring out the second. And twenty-eight years to win a Pulitzer. He has translated Russian poets, including Mandelstam, Yevtushenko, Akhmatova, and Akhmadulina. *I have walked through many lives,/some of them my own,/and I am not who I was,/though some principle of being/abides, from which I struggle/not to stray.*

Joanne KYGER (1934) arrived in San Francisco in 1957 and dropped in at a bar, The Place, frequented by Beat poets, and fell in with the crowd, Gary Snyder, Jack Spicer, Allen Ginsberg, and all. Her life with Snyder in the Far East is described in *Japan and India Journals 1960–64*. She lives in Bolinas, on the coast north of S.F. Her poems are collected in *Going On: selected poems, 1958–1980* and in various chapbooks and broadsides. *Writing for me is a kind of daily practice. Even if you don't have anything to say, you keep your hand in—that's the journal, just jotting something down, observations of the eternal weather. . . . thoughts and words can drift through you but once you write them down, they've arrived. And when something beautiful arrives, you want to have enough coordination to transcribe it.*

D. H. LAWRENCE (1885–1930) was the son of a miner in Nottinghamshire, infected with TB from childhood, encouraged to write by his mother. The success of his first novel, *The White Peacock* (1911), confirmed him as a writer, and the following year, he eloped with a married woman, Frieda von Richthofen (a cousin of the baron), and they traveled in Europe as he wrote *Sons and Lovers*. His third novel, *The Rainbow*, brought him under prosecution for obscenity, and he left England for Italy, then America, and Mexico, and finally back to Italy to die. *Lady Chatterley's Lover* was printed privately in Florence in 1928, which led to further prosecution. *Morality which is based on ideas, or on an ideal, is an unmitigated evil. No absolute is going to make the lion lie down with the lamb unless the lamb is inside. It is no good casting out devils. They belong to us, we must accept them and be at peace with them.*

Robert LAX (1915–2000) grew up in Queens, went to Columbia, converted to Catholicism, moved to Europe in the fifties, and settled on the Greek island of Patmos, a mysterious tall bearded man scarcely known in the poetry world, unanthologized, an unlisted number. A minimalist of the first water, his poem "River" consists of that single word repeated twelve times vertically on the page. *This is our camp, our moving city; each day we set the show up; jugglers calm amid currents, riding the world, juggled but slightly as in a howdah, on the grey wrinkled earth we ride as on an elephant's head.* His correspondence with his classmate Thomas Merton is collected in *A Catch of Anti-Letters.*

Mary LEADER (1948, Pawnee, OK) is a lawyer and a former Assistant Attorney General of Oklahoma who began writing poems in midcareer and switched from law to teaching literature, while earning a Ph.D. from Brandeis with a dissertation on Muriel Rukeyser.

David LEE (1944, Matador, TX) is a teacher, pig farmer, and runner in southern Utah.

Li-Young LEE (1957, Jakarta, Indonesia) was born of Chinese parents who brought him to this country as a small child. Author of *The City in Which I Love You, Book of My Nights,* and *The Winged Seed: A Remembrance.*

Ursula K. LEGUIN (1929, Berkeley) grew up in academia (the daughter of an anthropologist and a writer), married a historian, and began writing stories, then turned toward science fiction, for which she is best known.

Denise LEVERTOV (1923–1997) was born in Essex, England, settled in London, married an American, moved to New York and then to California, and spent the last ten years of her life in Seattle, within sight of Mount Rainier, her last great inspiration. Her father was a Hasidic Jew who became an Anglican parson. She was an early disciple of W. C. Williams and the Imagists and finished her career writing explicitly Christian poems. *Writing is a form of prayer.*

April LINDNER (1962, Hempstead, NY) is the author of *Skin. I'm most interested in the place beyond words, in trying to use words to get to the unsayable. I feel most fully engaged as a writer when I'm struggling with experiences that resist being put into words. Language on the page can't help being abstract, and I'm often frustrated with that abstraction, and wish I could dance or paint—anything that appeals to the senses more immediately than words on paper. I use this longing as a source of tension in my poems, trying to find words that engage the mind's ear and eye (and nose, tongue and fingertips) almost as surely as a more sensuous medium like dance, painting or music can.*

Gerald LOCKLIN (1941, Rochester, NY) is a prolific satirist and poet who teaches in Long Beach.

Guy W. LONGCHAMPS (1942, Anoka, MN) is the manager of Brock's Soda Fountain in Anoka and a driver on the Anoka-Minneapolis bus line.

Orval LUND (1940, Fargo, ND) teaches English in Winona, Minnesota, where he also fishes and hunts deer and edits the online poetry journal *Deep Breath.* Having been assigned to teach creative writing, he thought he should write what he was assigning his students to write and thus wrote his first poems.

Thomas LUX (1946, Northampton, MA) is the only child of a milkman and a switchboard operator. He grew up spending hours in the town library and started writing poems by imitating the ones on the back of Bob Dylan's albums. He started to think of himself as a poet in his junior year of college. *Given where I come from, I probably shouldn't be a poet. So I think I'm lucky.*

Walter MCDONALD (1934, Lubbock, TX) was an air force pilot whose first poems were written, he said, as letters to friends who died in Vietnam. His first memory of language was listening to his grandmother read poetry and Bible stories as he, four years old, lay propped up on an elbow, unaware that she was dying of cancer.

Louis MACNEICE (1907–1963), a Belfast boy, son of an Anglican rector, was a friend of Auden's, a teacher of Greek and philosophy, and for twenty years a staff writer for the BBC in 1941 in London. He wrote radio plays and poetry, and translated Goethe and Aeschylus. On location for the BBC, he descended into a mineshaft, caught pneumonia, and died just before his collection, *The Burning Perch*, was published. *Good-bye now, Plato and Hegel, the shop is closing down.*

Don MARQUIS (1878–1937) was a columnist for the New York *Sun*, where he introduced the cockroach Archie, a reincarnation of a poet laureate, and the free-spirited cat Mehitabel. *Happiness is the interval between periods of unhappiness.*

Herman MELVILLE (1819–1891) was a whaling novelist whose masterpiece (loved by some, considered unreadable by others) *Moby-Dick* was written in about a year at Melville's farm near Pittsfield, MA. The poor reception accorded his great work cost Melville dearly, and his work tailed off—another novel followed, some stories, and toward the end of his life, *Billy Budd*—during which he lived in obscurity in New York, a customs inspector.

William MEREDITH (1919, New York City) graduated from Princeton into the U.S. Navy, where he flew planes, and his first book of poems came out in 1944. He taught at Connecticut College for many years.

W. S. MERWIN (1927, New York City) has made his way in the world as a poet and translator (French, Spanish, Portuguese, Latin) and resides in a little jungly paradise in Hawaii, on a hillside on which he has planted hundreds of palm trees. *There was a period in the late fifties when I knew perfectly well I wasn't going to write for awhile. There wasn't anything I could write that didn't seem to me to be simply a continuation of what I'd been writing before. I didn't want to do that. I had to come to the end of a way of doing something.*

Robert MEZEY (1935, Philadelphia) served in the army and worked as a probation officer, ad writer, and social worker before entering the teaching business. For more than twenty years he was at Pomona College in the hills overlooking Los Angeles.

Edna St. Vincent MILLAY (1892–1950) was the shining red-haired heroine of bohemian fame in the twenties, famous for her excesses and not for her elegant formal verse.

Chuck MILLER (1939, Illinois). A Google search for "Chuck Miller" will show you how many Chucks and Millers and Chuck Millers there are in America, coaches and ag teachers and Baptist ministers, insurance men, DJs—fitting for a brilliant prairie proletarian poet (*Crossing the Kattegat, Northern Fields*) to be so much a part of his time. He has lived in Denmark, Czechoslovakia, Siberia, Indiana, Iowa, and worked as a dishwasher, ditchdigger, and teacher. *The thing I don't want . . . is a bunch of crap about my degrees, or who I studied with, or my M.F.A. from the University of Iowa blah-blah-blah, like you see on the back of so many books, particularly since I ended up absolute enemies with the Writer's Workshop; it would be ironic, galling, and disgusting to be identified as some product or protégé of theirs.*

Vassar MILLER (1924–1998) lived in Houston, a formalist poet, a passionately devout Christian, a woman who coped with cerebral palsy all her life. *Pity is a distraction, I'm too mean to die.*

Thomas MOORE (1779–1852) is the author of *Irish Melodies* (1807), which included many lyrics later mistaken for folk songs, "The Minstrel

Boy To The War Is Gone" and "Believe Me If All Those Endearing Young Charms" and "Tis The Last Rose of Summer" and others.

Frederick MORGAN (1922, New York City) is the founder and editor of the *Hudson Review*. *The poem comes as a gift. The best you can do with your will power is to keep the channel clear. For me, a life in which I have some kind of spiritual centering, meditation and prayer, is a way to keep the channel clear.*

Robert MORGAN (1944, Hendersonville, NC) is a scholar of Appalachian folklore and history whose novels set in western Carolina have attracted millions of readers, including *Gap Creek* and *The Truest Pleasure*. *Sinners make better characters.*

Howard MOSS (1922–1987) was the poetry editor of *The New Yorker* from 1950 until shortly before his death.

Lisel MUELLER (1924, Hamburg) came to the U.S. when she was fifteen, her father forced to flee the Nazis. In her poem "When I Am Asked," she describes how the death of her mother at the age of fifty-four moved her to write poetry. She lives in Lake Forest, Illinois.

James Ball NAYLOR (1860–1945) was a physician and humorist in Malta, Ohio, where he read a poem at the dedication of the Malta-McConnelsville steel bridge in 1902.

Howard NEMEROV (1920–1991) served in the R.C.A.F. and the U.S. Army Air Force in World War II and immediately after the war began teaching, first at Bennington, then at Washington University in St. Louis. He was a gifted writer who turned from fiction to plays to poetry to criticism with dazzling panache. *The only way out is the way through, just as you cannot escape from death except by dying. Being unable to write, you must examine in writing this being unable, which becomes for the present—henceforth?—the subject to which you are condemned.*

Harry NEWMAN, JR. (1921, St. Louis), of Harvard '42, has developed many malls and shopping centers out West, and has developed graduate programs in shopping center management.

Frank O'HARA (1926–1966) was the jumpy ebullient jazzy good-hearted poetry maitre'd of Manhattan until his tragic death—struck by a car on Fire Island. *Mothers of America, let your children go to the movies.*

Sharon OLDS (1942, San Francisco) went to Stanford, then leaped the country to attend Columbia and settled near there, on the Upper West Side of New York. Her first book was *Satan Says* in 1980.

Mary OLIVER (1935, Maple Heights, Ohio) lives in Vermont and Cape Cod. She worked at her writing for twenty-five years before publishing a book, rising at 5 A.M., avoiding writing workshops and such, avoiding interesting jobs lest she be distracted from her mission. *My school was the great poets: I read, and I read, and I read. I imitated—shamelessly, fearlessly. I was endlessly discontent. I looked at words and couldn't believe the largess of their sound—the whole sound structure of stops and sibilants, and things which I speak about now with students! All such mechanics have always fascinated me.*

John ORMOND (1923) was Welsh born and bred (Dunvant, in Glamorgan), the son of a shoemaker. He was a journalist and filmmaker and his *Definition of a Waterfall* was hailed as one of the best books of poems in the seventies.

Thomas Alan ORR has achieved an enviable degree of privacy, so that researchers have failed to unearth any details about him except that he is a social worker and lives somewhere in rural America.

Grace PALEY (1922, New York City) is a bard of Jewish New York and the author of phenomenal books like *The Little Disturbances of Man* and *Enormous Changes at the Last Minute*. She taught at Sarah Lawrence for years.

Linda PASTAN (1932, New York City) grew up in the Bronx, near the intersection of Fordham Road and the Grand Concourse, near Alexander's Department Store and Poe's cottage, the granddaughter of Jewish immigrants from eastern Europe. *The Last Uncle* is her most recent book, preceded by *Carnival Evening*, *An Early Afterlife*, and *Heroes in Disguise*.

Robert PHILLIPS lives in Houston and is the author of twenty-five books, *Spinach Days* and *News About People You Know* being his most recent.

Marge PIERCY (1936, Detroit) is a poet and novelist and lives by a marsh on Cape Cod with a husband and several cats. She has published fourteen books of poetry, including *To Be Of Use*, *Circles on the Water*, and *The Art of Blessing the Day: Poems with a Jewish Theme*. Her fifteen novels include *Three Women*, *The Longings of Women*, and *He, She and It*. *When I was young, I treated myself as a totally renewable resource. I slept little, smoked heavily, pushed myself. I would get up at six, write for four hours, go to three political meetings and a demonstration, make forty phone calls, cook supper for a gang of ten and dance all night and get up the next day and do it again. . . . When my health broke, when I came to the end of my energy and had to face my limits, I learned to be gentler, easier, quieter. . . . The happier I am, the better I work.*

Anne PORTER is the author of *An Altogether Different Language: Poems 1934–1994.*

Sheenagh PUGH (1950) lives in Cardiff, Wales, and writes fiction and poems and also translates, mainly from German.

Lawrence RAAB (1946, Pittsfield, MA) is a screenwriter and playwright, translator, critic, and essayist.

Barbara RAS (1949, New Bedford, MA) lives in Georgia. She has traveled widely in Latin America and lived in Costa Rica and edited a collection of Costa Rican fiction. Her first book of poems was *Bite Every Sorrow* in 1998.

Kenneth REXROTH (1905–1982) was born to an Indiana family of socialists and freethinkers, a self-educated man who painted, worked in theater, and wrote poems about *sex, mysticism, and revolution.* He moved easily from the Chicago radical scene of the thirties to the San Francisco Beat scene of the late fifties. In *An Autobiographical Novel,* he describes his youthful travels in the West and to Paris. He said he settled in San Francisco because it was not settled by Puritans but by *gamblers, prostitutes, rascals and fortune seekers,* and also because it was close to the mountains, where he loved to spend months at a time.

Theodore ROETHKE (1908–1963) was the son of a greenhouse owner in Saginaw, Michigan, and greenhouses and growers loom up often in his poems. He was an extraordinary teacher, while struggling with bipolar disorder, and an intensely private and introspective man behind his gaudy exterior of hoofer/pugilist/scatback/bullroarer/gangster. Interviewing for a teaching job once, he said, "I may look like a beer salesman, but I'm a poet." In the midfifties, traveling through Europe with his wife Beatrice, he wrote a batch of new poems, published in *Words for the Wind,* including his famous "I Knew a Woman Lovely in Her Bones." Once, he told a writing class to watch what he did so they could describe it accurately and he proceeded to climb out the window and walk along the fourth-story ledge and climb back in the window. He died of a heart attack after diving into a swimming pool while visiting friends at Bainbridge Island, WA. *Art is the means we have of undoing the damage of haste. It's what everything else isn't. You must believe: a poem is a holy thing—a good poem, that is. . . . I think of myself as a poet of love, a poet of praise, and I wish to be read aloud.*

Liz ROSENBERG teaches at SUNY Binghamton and her poems are collected in *These Happy Eyes, Children of Paradise* and *The Fire Music*. She has written numerous books for children, including *Earth-Shattering Poems* and *The Silence in the Mountains*.

Kay RYAN (1945) is a lifelong Californian and, for thirty years, an English teacher in Marin County. Her books include *Flamingo Watching, Elephant Rocks*, and *Say Uncle*. *Is there a sensation more exquisite than the feeling of having the burden of oneself borne off by a poem?*

May SARTON (1912–1995) grew up in Belgium and Cambridge, Mass., lived in a village in New Hampshire, and then on the Maine coast. She was the only child of a historian and a designer. She wrote memoirs (*Plant Dreaming Deep, Journal of a Solitude*), nineteen novels (*Mrs. Stevens Hears the Mermaids Singing*, in which she came out as a lesbian), and journals (*At Seventy, Endgame, Encore, At Eighty-Two*)—more than forty books in all. An actress in her youth, she did long annual tours, starting in 1940, giving readings and lectures, and made annual trips to Europe (she was fluent in French). *The lines run through my head and I can't stop them. I'd have to get up in the middle of the night and write them all down. They just flow through me.*

Steve SCAFIDI is a West Virginian, a cabinetmaker, and author of *Sparks from a Nine-Pound Hammer*.

Jim SCHLEY (1956, Milwaukee) was a book editor and a stilt-walker in the Bread and Puppet theater. He and his wife and daughter live in a home they built on a land cooperative in central Vermont.

Anne SEXTON (1928–1974) grew up in *comfortable* surroundings in Weston, MA, which made her distinctly uneasy—her father's alcoholism, her mother's anger—a tall, beautiful, dark-haired girl (later a fashion model) who eloped at nineteen and settled into a life of child-rearing, depression, and attempts at suicide. Her therapist suggested she try writing, and she did, and in 1960 her first collection (*To Bedlam and Part Way Back*) came out to favorable reviews. She became remarkably successful in a very short time, publishing four more books and winning a Pulitzer in 1967, even as her life unraveled, ravaged by alcoholism and depression. *The Death Notebooks* came out in 1974, and one day, in October of that year, after lunch with an old friend, she sat in her car in her closed garage in Boston, the engine running, and died.

William SHAKESPEARE (1564–1616) was a young man of twenty-three from the village of Stratford who went to London to act on the stage with The Queen's Company, then The Lord Chamberlain's Men, and, because there was an avid audience for such things, he wrote seventeen comedies, ten historical plays, and ten tragedies, prospering at his trade so that, by 1599, he owned a 10 percent share in The Globe theater. In 1609, the *Sonnets* came out. In addition to writing the plays, he cleverly disguised himself as Edward de Vere, 17th Earl of Oxford, and helped Francis Bacon with his *The Advancement of Learning*, and shot Christopher Marlowe just to watch him die. Shakespeare saw the defeat of the Spanish Armada, the death of Elizabeth I, two plagues, the discovery of the Gunpowder Plot, and the first English settlements of North America. *In winter's tedious nights sit by the fire with good old folks, and let them tell thee tales of woeful ages, long ago betid.*

Charles SIMIC (1938, Belgrade) was brought to the U.S. as a boy and grew up in Chicago, then moved to New York, went to night school, hung out with writers, did all sorts of jobs. He began writing poems, submitted them to magazines, collected them in books, and slowly accumulated a career. He wrote about himself in *An Unsentimental Education*. He is the author of more than sixty books. In an interview, asked if he ever sat down to write about a specific thing, Simic said, *Nope.* Asked if he ever wrote spontaneously, he said, *Sure, all the time.*

Louis SIMPSON (1923, Kingston, Jamaica) has written a dozen books of poems and as many of prose, including fiction, criticism, and a memoir.

Hal SIROWITZ (1949, New York City) is a popular performance artist at clubs and poetry slams. *His Mother Said* was about his late mother Estelle; he once said that the highest compliment he got was people telling him, *We must've had the same mother.*

David R. SLAVITT (1935, White Plains, NY) is a poet, novelist, and a writer of potboilers (under the pseudonym Henry Sutton), which put his children through school. *I rather like being ignored, having by now be-*

come accustomed to the freedom and the privacy that are the hand-
maidens to obscurity. I've come to understand that the lit biz is a silly
waste of time. Literature, on the other hand, is not.

Stevie SMITH (1902–1971) was a secretary at a publishing house in
London for thirty years, an occasional writer for the BBC, who came to
general attention in the UK only with the publication of her *Selected Po-*
ems when she was sixty.

Gary SNYDER (1930, San Francisco) is the bridge between the Beats
and the backpackers, whose first book, *Riprap* (1959), grew out of his experiences as a laborer at Yosemite and a lookout ranger. Snyder says that
one should live in one place, as an environmentally friendly deed, and
know the native plants and animals and where your water comes from.

William STAFFORD (1914–1993) migrated from Kansas to Iowa to
Oregon, where he taught for thirty-two years at Lewis and Clark College. Dreamy and good-hearted and ironical, his writing is not easily
mistaken for anyone else's. *Successful people can't write poems.*

Gerald STERN (1925, Pittsburgh) has won a mantelful of awards and
fellowships and grants, and nonetheless he writes fine poems indeed,
perhaps because he grew up in Pittsburgh, shooting pool, drinking beer,
playing football, dancing, and writing poetry, and didn't realize that poetry was the odd one.

Wallace STEVENS (1879–1955) was vice president of the Hartford Accident and Indemnity Co. and wrote poems on his way to and from the
office.

Robert Louis STEVENSON (1850–1894) grew up respectable in Edin-
burgh, the son of a lighthouse engineer. He himself tried engineering,
then law, before he left home to be a writer, traveling through Europe
and writing about it. Then to California in 1878, from which he wrote
The Amateur Emigrant. Magazine fiction followed, then, fortuitously, *Trea-*
sure Island, written to amuse his family and published in 1883, the real
start of his professional career, followed closely by *A Child's Garden of*
Verses, Kidnapped, Prince Otto, and his long short story, *Strange Case of Dr*
Jekyll and Mr Hyde. He arrived with his family in Samoa in 1889, and won
a few years reprieve from tuberculosis, died, and was buried at the top of
Mount Vaea under a stone with his poem inscribed: "Under the wide and
starry sky,/Dig the grave and let me lie . . ." Though admired by Henry

James, André Gide, Borges (who said that reading S. was "a form of happiness"), Brecht, Calvino, and others, R.L.S. was scorned by the Modernists and his literary stock sank steeply in the twentieth century. *Books are good enough in their own way, but they are a mighty bloodless substitute for life.*

Joseph STROUD studied at San Francisco State University and has taught for many years at Cabrillo. He is the author of *Below Cold Mountain*.

Joyce SUTPHEN grew up on a farm near St. Joseph, Minnesota. Her poems are collected in *Straight Out of View* and *Coming Back to the Body*.

May SWENSON (1913–1989) was born in May in Logan, Utah, the oldest of ten children of Mormon parents who emigrated from Sweden, and she moved to New York City as a young woman. She wrote poems about turtles, the subway, Long Island, football, space exploration, and, of course, death. *I am partly sensuous, but I also have a scientific bent. I want to know how things actually are.*

John TAGLIABUE (1923, Cantu, Italy) is the son of a restaurateur and has traveled widely in Europe, Mexico, and Japan.

Henry TAYLOR (1942, Loudoun County, VA) is a teacher, horseman, poet, parodist, and author of *Brief Candles*, a collection of clerihews including "According to Matthew/the wrath you/feel may be your own./ Live not by bread alone."

Sara TEASDALE (1884–1933) was born in Missouri, traveled in Europe, and made her home in New York City. At a time when poetry was expected to be somewhat overwrought, high-minded, in search of universals, she wrote simply and sparingly, starting with her first book, a collection of sonnets, in 1907. In poor health, alone in the city, she took an overdose of sleeping pills and died, a year after the suicide of her old lover, Vachel Lindsay.

Elizabeth THOMAS (1675–1731) wrote poems under the name "Corinna." In 1730, the Royal College of Physicians studied her case: she had swallowed a chicken bone in 1711 and suffered unpleasant after-effects for the rest of her life.

R. S. THOMAS (1913–2000) was a Welsh vicar at Eglwys-fach, Cardiganshire, and Aberdaron, Caernarfonshire, beside which church, St. Hywyn, where he was a priest for eleven years, his poem "The Other" is inscribed on slate ("There are nights that are so still/that I can hear the small owl calling/far off and a fox barking/miles away.") *There is a kind of narrowness in my work which a good critic would condemn.*

Henry David THOREAU (1817–1862) was a pencil maker and surveyor, a shy naturalist and woodsman, and canoeist for whom the town of Concord was more than big enough. He saw New York once and observed, "It must have a very bad influence on children to see so many human beings at once—mere herds of men." He conquered his timidity on the page, however, and blew his trumpet loud in *Walden, or Life in the Woods*. It was cobbled together from his journals, which came out in fourteen volumes in 1906. *A true account of the actual is the rarest poetry, for common sense always takes a hasty and superficial view.*

John UPDIKE (1932, Shillington, PA) grew up on an isolated farm, the son of a Lutheran science teacher in Shillington, the model for Updike's fictional towns of Olinger and Brewer, a landscape familiar to readers of *The Centaur* (1963) and the *Rabbit* quadrology (*R. Run, R. Redux, R. Is Rich*, and *R. at Rest*, followed by a novella, *R. Remembered*). A generous reviewer of fiction, a graceful and hugely prolific writer, he will observe, in 2005, Lord willing, half a century at *The New Yorker*. *Writing educates the writer as it goes along.*

David WAGONER (1926, Massillon, OH) is a novelist, working in the Western genre as well as mainstream fiction. He teaches at the University of Washington and edits *Poetry Northwest*.

Thom WARD (1963, Rochester, NY) is editor at BOA Editions and author of *Small Boat with Oars of Different Size*. He lives in Palmyra, NY.

Walt WHITMAN (1819–1892) was a volunteer nurse during the Civil War, a passage of his life beautifully rendered in Roy Morris, Jr.'s *The Better Angel: Walt Whitman in the Civil War.*

Reed WHITTEMORE (1919, New Haven) went to Yale, then to the army, then to Minnesota, where he taught at Carleton College, and then to Maryland. His titles include *An American Takes a Walk, The Fascination of the Abomination, Ways of Misunderstanding Poetry*, and *The Mother's Breast and the Father's House.*

Michael WIGGLESWORTH (1631–1705) was a doctor in Malden, MA, and also a Congregational minister, famous in his own day for a long religious poem, "The Day of Doom."

Richard WILBUR (1921, New York City) grew up in rural New Jersey, went to Amherst, bummed around the country (forty-six states) on freight trains and rode in a coal car over the Rockies, served in the army in the Italian campaign in Word War II. He is a translator (Molière), Broadway librettist (*Candide*), a poet of formal grace (after his hero John Milton), a founder (in 1959) of the important Wesleyan University Press poetry series. His *New and Collected Poems* came out in 1987. *In each art the difficulty of the form is a substitution for the difficulty of direct apprehension and expression of the object. The first difficulty may be more or less overcome, but the second is insuperable; thus every poem begins, or ought to, by a disorderly retreat to defensible positions. Or, rather, by a perception of the hopelessness of direct combat, and a resort to the warfare of spells, effigies, and prophecies. The relation between the artist and reality is an oblique one, and indeed there is no good art which is not consciously oblique. If you respect the reality of the world, you know that you can approach that reality only by indirect means.*

Ella Wheeler WILCOX (1850–1919) produced nearly forty volumes of poetry, poems about temperance, spirtualism, sentimental poems, which critics loved to scorn and millions of readers took to their collective bosom. Except for "Solitude," her work has mostly disappeared in the gentle mists.

Oscar WILDE (1854–1900) was the son of a Dublin physician and a woman poet, who went to Oxford, where he fell among the aesthetes ("Art for art's sake"), then to London, to find fame as a flamboyant character in a velvet coat and silk stockings and shoulder-length hair, then as a lecturer (across America, at the age of twenty-eight), and then as a successful playwright (*The Importance of Being Ernest*). He was jailed for two years, as a result of his love affair with Lord Alfred Douglas, to whom he wrote *De Profundis*. He wandered Europe for three years, sponging off friends, and wrote *The Ballad of Reading Gaol*, and died in Hotel d'Alsace in Paris, of cerebral meningitis. *When we are happy we are always good, but when we are good we are not always happy. To be good, according to the vulgar standards of goodness, is obviously quite easy. It merely requires a certain amount of sordid terror, a certain lack of imaginative thought and a certain low passion for middle-class respectability. Morality is simply the attitude we adopt towards people we personally dislike. The books that the world calls immoral are the books that show the world its own shame.*

C. K. WILLIAMS (1936, Newark, NJ) played college basketball and lived for many years in Philadelphia. He lives now in Princeton, NJ, and Paris.

Hugo WILLIAMS (1942, Windsor) lives in north London, teaches, reviews, writes for newspapers (*Freelancing: Adventures of a Poet*) and in 1962, traveled alone around the world and wrote about it in *All the Time in the World*. His *Billy's Rain* won the T. S. Eliot Prize in 2000. *I caught the Teheran Express to Aznow where the buses leave for Isfahan. It was easier than I'd thought. People imagine the obstacles mount as you get further from home, but the hardest country of all to travel in must be England, where everyone thinks you're barmy if you don't speak English in the local dialect.*

William Carlos WILLIAMS (1883–1963) was head pediatrician at the General Hospital in Paterson, NJ, and carried on a serious medical career delivering babies, and a parallel life as an avant-garde poet, a disciple of Ezra Pound, seeking to make poetry out of American speech, in works such as *Paterson*, published serially between 1946 and 1961, and *Pictures from Brueghel* (1962).

Charles WOLFE (1791–1823) was an Irish poet and curate. Sir John Moore was a commander of British light infantry in the Napoleonic wars, and was killed in the retreat to Corunna, in Spain, in 1809.

Baron WORMSER (1948, Baltimore) is a librarian in Madison, Maine. *Serious poetry is forceful and creates the feeling that something important is at hand. It represents something larger than any individual man or woman—community.*

James A. WRIGHT (1927–1980) was the son of a factory worker and grew up in bleak and blackened circumstances in Martins Ferry, OH, determined to leave and never return. He served in the U.S. Army, then went to Kenyon College on the G. I. bill, started writing seriously, was elected to Phi Beta Kappa, married his high school sweetheart, Liberty Kardules, won a Fulbright grant, and went off to Vienna, then took a doctorate at the University of Washington under Theodore Roethke. Hardy and Frost were heroes of his, and certain Chinese poets. His *The Branch Shall Not Break* was considered a major breakthrough in 1963. He wound up living in New York City, and the year before he died, of throat cancer, Wright had a supremely happy time traveling with his second wife Annie through Italy and France, moving from town to town, writing poems. *I don't believe in God. He hurts too much.*

W. B. YEATS (1865–1939), Dublin born, was a student of Irish mythology and mystical symbolism and the occult, a member of the Golden Dawn Society, and the editor of *Fairy and Folk Tales of the Irish Peasantry* (1888) and the author of many plays based on myth and legend. He fell in love with an Irish nationalist, Maud Gonne, who declined to marry him—though he wrote her a play to star in, *Cathleen ni Houlihan.* She was the great shining love of his life and of his poems. Along with his patron Lady Gregory and John Millington Synge, he was the backbone of the Irish Renaissance, which led to the founding of the Abbey Theatre. A reluctant politician (he was elected to the Irish Senate in 1922), he spent considerable time away from Ireland and died in the south of France. *All things can tempt me from this craft of verse.*

Paul ZIMMER (1934, Canton, OH) ran university presses at Pittsburgh, Georgia, and Iowa, then retired to his farm near Soldiers Grove, WI. Author of many collections, including *Family Reunion* and *The Great Bird of Love*. *Some people view life as food served by a psychopath. They do not trust it. But Zimmer expects always to be happy. Puzzled by melancholy, he pours a reward and loves this world relentlessly.*

Name Index

Andrews, Ginger, 180
Anonymous, 16–17, 122–23, 357, 361–63
Appleman, Philip, 12, 166–67, 374–75
Arnold, Bob, 159–60
Auden, W.H., 205–6, 345, 359

Barker, George, 416
Barnes, Kate, 360
Belloc, Hilaire, 185
Berry, Wendell, 236, 255, 274–75, 295, 371–72, 426
Berryman, John, 10–11
Bishop, Elizabeth, 35–36, 139–40, 186–87
Blake, William, 423
Blount, Roy, Jr., 330–31
Bly, Robert, 33, 221, 322, 358, 381
Booth, Philip, 153–55, 190, 245–46
Bryan, Sharon, 207–8
Budbill, David, 37, 225, 315, 428
Bukowski, Charles, 76–77, 217, 263, 277–78
Burns, Robert, 93, 113

Carruth, Hayden, 45, 204, 235, 350, 421
Carryl, Charles Edward, 293–94
Carver, Raymond, 8–9, 146, 149, 299, 393–95
Clare, John, 95, 126
Clark, Thomas A., 151–52
Collins, Billy, 48–49, 291–92
Cope, Wendy, 133

Cox, Jimmie, 262
cummings, e.e., 127

Dangel, Leo, 136
Daniells, Roy, 90
Davies, W. H., 216
Der-Hovanessian, Diana, 391–92
Dickinson, Emily, 34, 211, 230, 231, 253, 279, 305, 329
Disch, Tom, 276
Dischell, Stuart, 336
Dobyns, Stephen, 268, 338–39, 378
Douglas, Keith, 128–29
Dunn, Stephen, 131–32, 218, 223

Emerson, Ralph Waldo, 384–85
Ewart, Gavin, 89

Fairchild, B.H., 67–68
Ferlinghetti, Lawrence, 69–70, 414–15
Field, Edward, 40, 168–69
Frost, Robert, 66, 145, 289

Gallagher, Tess, 184
Gambino, Erica-Lynn, 110
Garrison, Deborah, 84–85
Gioia, Dana, 80–81
Gregg, Linda, 433
Guiterman, Arthur, 31

Hall, Donald, 161–62, 248–49, 313, 398, 403
Hanzlicek, C.G., 18–19, 178–79
Hass, Robert, 256, 261
Hayden, Robert, 369
Heaney, Seamus, 297

Hecht, Jennifer Michael, 106
Hedin, Robert, 370
Hendry, J.F., 105
Hennen, Tom, 32, 41
Hewitt, Geof, 259
Hirshfield, Jane, 430–31
Holm, Bill, 202–3
Hopkins, Gerard Manley, 432
Huddle, David, 60–61
Hughes, Langston, 400

Ignatow, David, 410
Irwin, Mark, 82–83

Jackson, Bessie (Lucille Bogan),
    270–71
Jarrell, Randall, 237–38
Jenkins, Louis, 116, 260
Jones, Richard, 107–8, 183
Jong, Erica, 347–48
Justice, Donald, 54, 73

Kasdorf, Julia, 156
Kennedy, X.J., 343–44
Kenyon, Jane, 25–26, 411–12, 417
Kerrigan, T.S., 327
Kingsley, Charles, 390
Kinnell, Galway, 4, 15
Kinsley, Robert, 290
Kumin, Maxine, 99–100, 194–95,
    241–42
Kunitz, Stanley, 346
Kyger, Joanne, 244

Lawrence, D.H., 55
Lax, Robert, 50
Leader, Mary, 53
Lee, David, 351–53
Lee, Li-Young, 427
Leguin, Ursula, 243
Levertov, Denise, 28
Lindner, April, 337
Locklin, Gerald, 272–73, 286
Longchamps, Guy W., 332–33
Longfellow, H.W., 287
Lund, Orval, 88
Lux, Thomas, 3, 74–75, 176

McDonald, Walter, 124–25
MacNeice, Louis, 257
Marquis, Don, 46–47
Melville, Herman, 284
Meredith, William, 27
Merwin, W.S., 285, 376–77, 413
Mezey, Robert, 379–80
Millay, Edna St. Vincent, 130, 397
Miller, Chuck, 312
Miller, Vassar, 30
Moore, Thomas, 111
Morgan, Frederick, 320
Morgan, Robert, 63, 373
Moss, Howard, 58–59, 141–42,
    303–4
Mueller, Lisel, 42, 120–21, 200–201,
    224, 316–18, 396

Naylor, James B(all), 389
Nemerov, Howard, 188–89, 199, 226,
    240
Newman, Harry, Jr., 354–55

O'Hara, Frank, 101
Olds, Sharon, 114, 367–68
Oliver, Mary, 222
Ormond, John, 356
Orr, Thomas Alan, 164–65

Paley, Grace, 429
Pastan, Linda, 175, 228, 399
Phillips, Robert, 56, 103–4
Piercy, Marge, 157–58
Porter, Anne, 405–6
Pugh, Sheenagh, 215

Raab, Lawrence, 181–82
Ras, Barbara, 191–92
Rexroth, Kenneth, 29, 138, 334
Roethke, Theodore, 298
Rosenberg, Liz, 134
Ryan, Kay, 173–74

Sarton, May, 306, 335, 382–83, 404
Scafidi, Steve, 143–44
Schley, Jim, 51–52

Sexton, Anne, 5–6, 213–14
Shakespeare, William, 177, 220
Simic, Charles, 23–24
Simpson, Louis, 112, 349
Sirowitz, Hal, 102
Slavitt, David R., 407
Smith, Stevie, 401
Snyder, Gary, 170
Stafford, William, 212, 283
Stern, Gerald, 193, 328
Stevens, Wallace, 309
Stevenson, Robert Louis, 64
Stroud, Joseph, 57, 296
Sutphen, Joyce, 163, 269
Swenson, May, 250

Tagliabue, John, 229, 258, 323
Taylor, Henry, 62, 78–79, 239
Teasdale, Sara, 137
Thomas, Elizabeth, 267
Thomas, R.S., 135
Thoreau, Henry David, 424–25
Trail, C.B., 97

Updike, John, 150, 247, 402

Wagoner, David, 219
Ward, Thom, 117–18
Whitman, Walt, 38–39, 94
Whittemore, Reed, 13, 86–87,
    119
Wigglesworth, Michael, 14
Wilbur, Richard, 307–8,
    319
Wilcox, Ella Wheeler, 254
Wilde, Oscar, 314
Williams, C.K., 65, 227
Williams, Hugo, 115
Williams, William Carlos,
    109
Wolfe, Charles, 408–9
Wormser, Baron, 310–11
Wright, James, 422

Yeats, W.B., 96, 98

Zimmer, Paul, 321

Title Index

Address to the Lord, 10–11
After the Argument, 131–32
After Forty Years of Marriage, She
    Tries a New Recipe for
    Hamburger Hot Dish, 136
After a Movie, 78–79
After Work, 183
Alley Violinist, 50
Animals, 101
Another Spring, 29
As Befits a Man, 400
At Last the Secret Is Out, 359
At Least, 8–9
At Twenty-Three Weeks She Can No
    Longer See Anything South of
    Her Belly, 117–18
August Third, 382–83
Authorship, 389

Bare Arms of Trees, The, 258
Bats, 237–38
Bess, 175
Birthday Card to My Mother, 374–75
Bison Crossing Near Mt. Rushmore,
    250
Blessing, A, 422
Bonnard's Nudes, 146
Bookmark, A, 276
Boy at the Window, 319
British Museum Reading Room, The,
    257
Burial of Sir John Moore after
    Corunna, The, 408–9

Cathedral Builders, 356
Changed Man, The, 103–4
Childhood, 191–92

Coming, 334
Comin thro' the Rye, 113
Confession, 268
Constant North, The, 105
Courage, 213–14
Cradle Song, 51–52

Dance, The, 65
Death and the Turtle, 404
December Moon, 306
Departures, 399
Destruction, 244
Dilemma, 37
Directions, 296
Dirge Without Music, 397
Dog's Death, 247
Dostoevsky, 76–77
Down in the Valley, 122–23
Dumka, The, 67–68

Ed, 349
Eel in the Cave, The, 221
Egg, 178–79
Eleanor's Letters, 403
Elevator Music, 62
Elvis Kissed Me, 327
Excelsior, 287
Excrement Poem, The, 241–42

Family Reunion, 194–95
Fantastic Names of Jazz, The, 204
Farmhouse, The, 86–87
Farm Wife, 135
Feast, The, 261
First Green of Spring, The, 428
First Kiss, 337
First Lesson, 190

First Love, 95
First time I remember waking up . . . ,
    255
Fishing in the Keep of Silence, 433
Flight, 116
For the Anniversary of My Death,
    413
For C.W.B., 139–40
For the Life of Him and Her, 119
For My Son, Noah, Ten Years Old,
    33
Forsaken Wife, The, 267
Forty-Five, 421
Four Poems in One, 405–6
Franklin Hyde, Who caroused in the
    Dirt and was corrected by His
    Uncle, 185
From Blossoms, 427
From the Manifesto of the Selfish,
    223

Girl on a Tractor, 163
Grain of Sound, The, 63

Happiness, 149
Hay for the Horses, 170
Her Door, 53
Here, 429
Her First Calf, 236
Her Long Illness, 313
He Wishes for the Cloths of Heaven,
    96
Hoeing, 150
Holy Thursday, 423
Homage: Doo-Wop, 57
Home on the Range, 16–17
Hope, 224
How Many Nights, 4
How to See Deer, 245–46

Iceberg Theory, The, 272–73
Icelandic Language, The, 202–3
I Go Back to May 1937, 367–68
in celebration of surviving, 312
In a Prominent Bar in Secaucus One
    Day, 343–44
Instrument of Choice, 56

Investment, The, 66
I shall keep singing! . . . , 329
I Stop Writing the Poem, 184
I've Known a Heaven . . . , 34
I Will Make You Brooches, 64

January, 310–11

Kaddish, 410

Landing Pattern, 166–67
last song, the, 263
Late Hours, 42
Lazy, 351–53
Leisure, 216
Lending Out Books, 102
Lester Tells of Wanda and the Big
    Snow, 321
Let Evening Come, 417
Letter to N.Y., 35–36
Life of a Day, The, 32
Light Left On, A, 335
Little Citizen, Little Survivor,
    235
Little Tooth, A, 176
Lives of the Heart, The, 430–31
Living, 28
Living in the Body, 269
Loft, The, 107–8
Lost, 219

Mae West, 168–69
Magellan Street, 1974, 99–100
Manifesto: The Mad Farmer Libera-
    tion Front, 274–75
Manners for a Child of 1918, 186–87
March Blizzard, 323
Master Speed, The, 145
Masterworks of Ming, 173–74
Mehitabel's Song, 46–47
Memory, 350
Middle Years, The, 124–25
Moby-Dick, from, 284
Moderation Is Not a Negation of
    Intensity, But Helps Avoid Mo-
    notony, 229
Morning Person, 30

Music One Looks Back On, The, 338–39
My Dad's Wallet, 393–95
My Life Before I Knew It, 181–82
My Mother, 379–80
My mother said, "Of course . . . , 398

Names of Horses, 248–49
New Hampshire, 303–4
New Yorkers, 40
Nightclub, 48–49
Night Journey, 298
Night Light, 360
Noah, 90
Nobody Knows You When You're Down and Out, 262
No Map, 378
Not Only the Eskimos, 316–18
No Tool or Rope or Pail, 159–60

Ode to the Medieval Poets, 205–6
O Karma, Dharma, pudding and pie, 12
Old Boards, 322
Old Italians Dying, *from*, 414–15
Old Liberators, The, 370
O Luxury, 332–33
Once in the 40s, 283
On the Strength of All Convictions and the Stamina of Love, 106
On a Tree Fallen Across the Road (To Hear Us Talk), 289
Ooly Pop a Cow, 60–61
Orange, The, 133
Otherwise, 25–26
Our Lady of the Snows, 256
Ox Cart Man, 161–62

Parable of the Four-Poster, 347–48
Passengers, 291–92
Peace of Wild Things, The, 426
Perfection Wasted, 402
Persistence of Song, The, 58–59
Piano, 55
Place for Everything, A, 260
Poem About Morning, 27

Poem to Be Read at 3 A.M., 73
Poem in Thanks, 3
poetry readings, 277–78
Politics, 98
Portrait, The, 346
Possessive Case, The, 200–201
Postscript, 297
Prayer for a Marriage, 143–44
Primer of the Daily Round, A, 199
Props assist the House, The, 231
Psalm, 13
Psalm 23, 7
Psalm 121, 14
Publication—is the Auction . . . , 279
Pupil, The, 54

Quietly, 138

Rain Travel, 285
Red, Red Rose, A, 93
Relations: Old Light/New Sun/Post-mistress/Earth/04421, 153–55
Repression, 227
Requiescat, 314
Riding Lesson, 239
Ritual to Read to Each Other, A, 212
Rolls-Royce Dreams, 180
Romantics: Johannes Brahms and Clara Schumann, 120–21
Routine, 31

Sailor, The, 259
Saturday Morning, 115
Scandal, The, 358
Scrambled Eggs and Whiskey, 45
Secret Life, A, 218
September, the First Day of School, 188–89
Shifting the Sun, 391–92
Shorelines, 141–42
Sir Patrick Spens, 361–63
Sixth of January, The, 315
Snow Man, The, 309
Soaking Up Sun, 41
Solitude, 254
Some Details of Hebridean House Construction, 151–52

Sometimes, 215
Song of Myself, *lines from,* 38–39
Song to Onions, 330–31
Sonnet, 97
Sonnet 25, 220
Sonnet XLIII, 130
Sonnet XXXVII, 177
Soybeans, 164–65
Spring, 432
Stanza IV *from* Coming of Age, 243
Stepping Out of Poetry, 328
Street Ballad, 416
Success is counted sweetest, 253
Summer Morning, 23–24, 112
Summer Storm, 80–81
Sunt Leones, 401
Susquehanna, 134
Sweater Weather: A Love Song to
    Language, 207–8
Swimming Pool, The, 74–75

Tell all the Truth but tell it slant . . . ,
    230
Terminus, 384–85
Testimonial, 354–55
This Is Just to Say (Gambino), 110
This Is Just to Say (Williams), 109
Those Who Love, 137
Those Winter Sundays, 369
Three Goals, The, 225
Tired As I Can Be, 270–71
Titanic, 407
To be of use, 157–58
To fight aloud is very brave . . . , 305
To My Mother, 371–72
Topography, 114
Twilight: After Haying, 411–12

Vacation, The, 295
Venetian Air, 111
Vergissmeinnicht, 128–29

Vermeer, 226
Village Burglar, The, 357

Waiting, 299
Walden, from, 424–25
Walk Along the Old Tracks, A, 290
Walking the Dog, 240
Walloping Window-Blind, The,
    293–94
Waving Good-Bye, 193
way it is now, the, 217
Weather, 228
We grow accustomed to the Dark . . . ,
    211
Welcome Morning, 5–6
What I Learned from My Mother,
    156
What I Want Is, 18–19
When I Am Asked, 396
When I Heard at the Close of Day,
    94
When My Dead Father Called, 381
When one has lived a long time
    alone, 15
where we are, 286
Who's Who, 345
Wild Geese, 222
Winter Poem, 320
Winter Winds Cold and Blea, 126
Woolworth's, 82–83
Worked Late on a Tuesday Night,
    84–85
Working in the Rain, 373
wrist-wrestling father, 88

Year's End, 307–8
Yellow Slicker, The, 336
Yesterday, 376–77
Yorkshiremen in Pub Gardens,
    89
Young and Old, 390

Thomas Allan Orr, "Soybeans" from *Hammers in the Fog*. Copyright © 1995 by Thomas Allan Orr. Reprinted with permission of the author and Restoration Press.

Grace Paley, "Here" from *Begin Again: Collected Poems*. Copyright © 2000 by Grace Paley. Reprinted by permission of Farrar, Straus and Giroux, LLC.

Linda Pastan, "Bess," "Practicing," and "Weather" from *Last Uncle*. Copyright © 2002 by Linda Pastan. "Departures" from *Carnival Evening: New and Selected Poems 1968–1998*. Copyright © 1998 by Linda Pastan. Used by permission of W. W. Norton & Company, Inc.

Robert Phillips, "The Changed Man" and "Instrument of Choice" from *Spinach Days*. Copyright © 2000 by Robert Phillips. Reprinted with permission of the Johns Hopkins University Press.

Marge Piercy, "To be of use" from *Circles on the Water*. Copyright © 1982 by Marge Piercy. Used by permission of Alfred A. Knopf, a division of Random House, Inc.

Anne Porter, "Four Poems in One" from *An Altogether Different Language*. Copyright © 1994 by Anne Porter. Reprinted with permission of Zoland Books, Cambridge, Massachusetts.

Sheenagh Pugh, "Sometimes" from *Selected Poems* (Dufour Editions, 1990). Reprinted with permission of Sheenagh Burns.

Lawrence Raab, "My Life Before I Knew It" from *The Probable World*. Copyright © Lawrence Raab, 2000. Reprinted with permission of Penguin Books, a division of Penguin Putnam Inc.

Barbara Ras, "Childhood" from *Bite Every Sorrow*. Copyright © 1998 by Barbara Ras. Reprinted by permission of Louisiana State University Press.

Kenneth Rexroth, "Another Spring" from *One Hundred Poems from the Chinese*. Copyright © 1971 by Kenneth Rexroth. "Coming" and "Quietly" from *Collected Shorter Poems*. Copyright © 1966, 1963, 1962, 1952, 1949, 1940 by Kenneth Rexroth. Copyright © 1956, 1951, 1950, 1944 by New Directions Publishing Corp. Reprinted by permission of New Directions Publishing Corp.

Theodore Roethke, "Night Journey" from *The Collected Poems of Theodore Roethke*. Copyright 1940 by Theodore Roethke. Used by permission of Doubleday, a division of Random House, Inc.

Liz Rosenberg, "Susquehanna" from *Children of Paradise*. Copyright © 1994 by Liz Rosenberg. Reprinted by permission of the University of Pittsburgh Press.

Kay Ryan, "Masterworks of Ming" from *Flamingo Watching*. Copyright © 1994 by Copper Beech Press. Used by permission.

May Sarton, "August Third," "Death and the Turtle," and "A Light Left On" from *Collected Poems 1930–1993*. Copyright © 1993, 1988, 1984, 1980, 1974 by May Sarton. "December Moon" from *Coming into Eighty*. Copyright © 1994 by May Sarton. Used by permission of W. W. Norton & Company, Inc.

Steve Scafidi, "Prayer for a Marriage" from *Sparks from a Nine–Pound Hammer*. Copyright © 2001 by Steve Scafidi. Reprinted by permission of Louisiana State University Press.

Jim Schley, "Cradle Song" from *One Another* (Chapiteau Press, Montpelier, Vermont, 1999). (www.chapiteau.org) Used with permission of the author.

Anne Sexton, "Courage" and "Welcome Morning" from *The Awful Rowing Toward God*. Copyright © 1975 by Loring Conant, Jr., Executor of the Estate of Anne Sexton. Reprinted by permission of Houghton Mifflin Company. All rights reserved.

Charles Simic, "Summer Morning" from *Charles Simic: Selected Early Poems*. Copyright © 1999 by Charles Simic. Reprinted by permission of George Braziller, Inc.

Louis Simpson, "Ed" from *The Best Hour of the Night* (Ticknor & Fields). Copyright © 1983 by Louis Simpson. "Summer Morning" from *At the End of the Open Road* (Wesleyan University Press). Copyright © 1963 by Louis Simpson. Reprinted by permission of Louis Simpson.

Hal Sirowitz, "Lending Out Books" from *My Therapist Said* (Crown Publishers). Copyright © 1998 by Hal Sirowitz. Reprinted with permission of the Joy Harris Literary Agency.

David R. Slavitt, "Titanic" from *Big Nose*. Copyright © 1983 by David R. Slavitt. Reprinted by permission of Louisiana State University Press.

Stevie Smith, "Sunt Leones" from *Collected Poems of Stevie Smith*. Copyright © 1972 by Stevie Smith. Reprinted by permission of New Directions Publishing Corp.

Gary Snyder, "Hay for the Horses" from *Riprap and Cold Mountain Poems*. Copyright © 1990 by Gary Snyder. Reprinted by permission of Farrar, Straus and Giroux, LLC.

William Stafford, "Once in the 40s" copyright © 1982, 1998 by the Estate of William Stafford. "A Ritual to Read to Each Other"copyright © 1960, 1998 by the Estate of William Stafford. From *The Way It Is: New and Selected Poems*. Reprinted with permission of Graywolf Press, Saint Paul, Minnesota.

Gerald Stern, "Stepping Out of Poetry" copyright © 1998 by Gerald Stern. "Waving Good-Bye" copyright © 1981 by Gerald Stern. From *This Time: New and Selected Poems*. Used by permission of W. W. Norton & Company, Inc.

Wallace Stevens, "The Snow Man" from *The Collected Poems of Wallace Stevens*. Copyright 1954 by Wallace Stevens and renewed 1982 by Holly Stevens. Used by permission of Alfred A. Knopf, a division of Random House, Inc.

Joseph Stroud, "Directions" and "Homage: Doo-Wop" from *Below Cold Mountain*. Copyright © 1998 by Joseph Stroud. Reprinted with permission of Copper Canyon Press, P.O. Box 271, Port Townsend, Washington 98368-0271.

Joyce Sutphen, "Girl on a Tractor" from *Coming Back to the Body*, Holy Cow! Press, 2000. Reprinted by permission of Holy Cow! Press and the author.